PaaS Mastery
Platform as a Service

Your All-In-One Guide To Azure Pipelines, Google Cloud, Microsoft Azure, And IBM Cloud

4 BOOKS IN 1

BOOK 1
PaaS Mastery: Navigating Azure Pipelines and Beyond

BOOK 2
Cloud Powerhouse: Mastering PaaS with Google, Azure, and IBM

BOOK 3
Platform as a Service Unleashed: A Comprehensive Guide to Google Cloud, Microsoft Azure, and IBM Cloud

BOOK 4
From Novice to Pro: PaaS Mastery Across Azure Pipelines, Google Cloud, Microsoft Azure, and IBM Cloud

ROB BOTWRIGHT

Published by Rob Botwright
Library of Congress Cataloging-in-Publication Data
ISBN 978-1-83938-591-9
Cover design by Rizzo

Disclaimer

The contents of this book are based on extensive research and the best available historical sources. However, the author and publisher make no claims, promises, or guarantees about the accuracy, completeness, or adequacy of the information contained herein. The information in this book is provided on an "as is" basis, and the author and publisher disclaim any and all liability for any errors, omissions, or inaccuracies in the information or for any actions taken in reliance on such information. The opinions and views expressed in this book are those of the author and do not necessarily reflect the official policy or position of any organization or individual mentioned in this book. Any reference to specific people, places, or events is intended only to provide historical context and is not intended to defame or malign any group, individual, or entity. The information in this book is intended for educational and entertainment purposes only. It is not intended to be a substitute for professional advice or judgment. Readers are encouraged to conduct their own research and to seek professional advice where appropriate. Every effort has been made to obtain necessary permissions and acknowledgments for all images and other copyrighted material used in this book. Any errors or omissions in this regard are unintentional, and the author and publisher will correct them in future editions.

Book 1 - PaaS Mastery: Navigating Azure Pipelines and Beyond

Book 2 - Cloud Powerhouse: Mastering PaaS with Google, Azure, and IBM

Book 3 - Platform as a Service Unleashed: A Comprehensive Guide to Google Cloud, Microsoft Azure, and IBM Cloud

Book 4 - From Novice to Pro: PaaS Mastery Across Azure Pipelines, Google Cloud, Microsoft Azure, and IBM Cloud

Introduction

Welcome to "PaaS Mastery: Your All-In-One Guide To Azure Pipelines, Google Cloud, Microsoft Azure, And IBM Cloud." In today's fast-paced digital landscape, cloud computing has become the cornerstone of innovation and agility for organizations worldwide. Among the various cloud service models, Platform as a Service (PaaS) stands out as a transformative force, empowering businesses to develop, deploy, and scale applications with unprecedented ease and efficiency.

This comprehensive book bundle comprises four distinct volumes, each dedicated to unraveling the intricacies of PaaS and its implementation across the cloud ecosystems of Azure Pipelines, Google Cloud, Microsoft Azure, and IBM Cloud. Together, these volumes offer a holistic, in-depth exploration of PaaS, providing you with a comprehensive understanding of this game-changing technology.

Book 1 - "PaaS Mastery: Navigating Azure Pipelines and Beyond" lays the foundation for your PaaS journey. We start by demystifying Azure Pipelines, Microsoft's robust PaaS offering, and then expand our horizons to explore the broader Azure ecosystem. With hands-on guidance, best practices, and real-world examples, you'll learn how to harness the power of Azure PaaS to streamline your application development and deployment processes.

In Book 2 - "Cloud Powerhouse: Mastering PaaS with Google, Azure, and IBM," we broaden our scope to encompass the PaaS offerings of three cloud powerhouses: Google Cloud, Microsoft Azure, and IBM Cloud. These giants have redefined the landscape of cloud computing, and this volume equips you with the knowledge to leverage their respective PaaS platforms effectively.

Book 3 - "Platform as a Service Unleashed: A Comprehensive Guide to Google Cloud, Microsoft Azure, and IBM Cloud" takes a deep dive into the unique features and capabilities of each cloud provider's PaaS offerings. Whether you're a developer, IT professional, or decision-maker, this book serves as a valuable reference guide to help you make informed choices about the platform that aligns best with your organization's needs.

Finally, in Book 4 - "From Novice to Pro: PaaS Mastery Across Azure Pipelines, Google Cloud, Microsoft Azure, and IBM Cloud," we adopt a holistic approach to PaaS mastery. Here, we explore the art of optimizing PaaS applications, combining the strengths of multiple cloud platforms, and advancing from a novice to a pro in the realm of cloud computing.

Throughout this book bundle, we'll dive into various facets of PaaS, including application development, deployment strategies, containerization, microservices architecture, security best practices, compliance *requirements, emerging technologies, and the future of PaaS development. The world of cloud computing is constantly evolving, and PaaS is at the forefront of this transformation. Whether you're embarking on your PaaS journey or looking to enhance your existing skills, this bundle is designed to empower you with the knowledge and expertise needed to navigate the complex landscape of PaaS successfully.*

So, prepare to embark on a journey of discovery, innovation, and mastery as we delve into the world of Platform as a Service with "PaaS Mastery: Your All-In-One Guide To Azure Pipelines, Google Cloud, Microsoft Azure, And IBM Cloud." Let's unlock the full potential of PaaS together.

BOOK 1
PaaS Mastery
Navigating Azure Pipelines and Beyond

ROB BOTWRIGHT

Chapter 1: Introduction to Platform as a Service (PaaS)

Platform as a Service, commonly known as PaaS, stands as a pivotal concept in the realm of cloud computing and software development, representing a powerful solution for developers and businesses alike. To truly comprehend the significance of PaaS, one must delve into its fundamental principles and grasp the intricacies that define its function within the broader cloud ecosystem. PaaS, in essence, offers a comprehensive framework that empowers developers to create, deploy, and manage applications without the hassles of managing the underlying infrastructure. This liberating approach frees developers from the burdens of server provisioning, hardware maintenance, and software updates, allowing them to focus their energy on innovation and coding.

At its core, PaaS provides a development environment that streamlines the entire application lifecycle, from conception and coding to testing, deployment, and ongoing management. This unified platform encompasses tools, services, and resources that cater to various development needs, fostering collaboration and agility within development teams. Unlike Infrastructure as a Service (IaaS), where users manage virtualized hardware resources, or Software as a Service (SaaS), where users consume pre-built software applications, PaaS strikes a balance by offering the middle ground—a platform for building custom applications tailored to specific business requirements.

Intriguingly, the evolution of PaaS has mirrored the broader trends in cloud computing, adapting to meet the demands of modern software development practices. It has grown from a simple concept to a multifaceted ecosystem encompassing a myriad of services and providers, each catering to distinct use cases and industries. Google Cloud Platform (GCP), Microsoft Azure, IBM Cloud, and other major cloud providers have all developed their PaaS offerings, adding layers of complexity and sophistication to the PaaS landscape.

One of the key tenets of PaaS revolves around its role in abstracting the underlying infrastructure. By doing so, PaaS reduces the complexity and overhead associated with traditional software development, allowing developers to focus solely on their code. This abstraction extends to various facets of application development, including database management, server provisioning, and networking. As a result, developers can leverage pre-built components, libraries, and services provided by the PaaS platform, accelerating development cycles and enhancing overall productivity.

However, PaaS is not a one-size-fits-all solution; rather, it caters to a diverse range of applications, from web and mobile apps to microservices and IoT applications. The versatility of PaaS platforms allows developers to choose the tools and services that align with their specific project requirements. For example, a web application developer might leverage PaaS offerings for web hosting, databases, and content delivery, while a data scientist could utilize PaaS tools for big data analytics and machine learning.

To fully harness the power of PaaS, it's crucial to understand the advantages it brings to the table. First and foremost, PaaS fosters collaboration among development teams by providing a centralized environment for code sharing and version control. This collaborative approach streamlines the development process, ensuring that multiple developers can work on a project simultaneously without conflicts or disruptions. Moreover, PaaS platforms often integrate with popular development tools like Git and Jenkins, further enhancing team efficiency.

Another significant benefit of PaaS is its ability to auto-scale applications based on demand. This dynamic scaling ensures that applications can handle fluctuations in user traffic and workload, optimizing resource utilization and cost-efficiency. Developers can configure auto-scaling rules and policies to adapt the application's capacity in real-time, reducing the need for manual intervention.

Furthermore, PaaS encourages a DevOps culture by blurring the lines between development and operations. With PaaS, developers have more control over the deployment and management of their applications, fostering a sense of ownership and accountability. This shift in mindset promotes collaboration between developers and operations teams, leading to faster deployment cycles and higher-quality applications.

PaaS also plays a crucial role in ensuring the security and compliance of applications. Most PaaS providers offer built-in security features and compliance certifications, helping organizations meet regulatory requirements and protect sensitive data. These security measures include encryption, identity and access management, and threat detection, among others.

In addition to security, PaaS platforms provide robust monitoring and analytics capabilities. These tools allow developers to gain real-time insights into the performance of their applications, helping them identify and address issues promptly. Monitoring dashboards, logs, and alerts enable proactive troubleshooting, reducing downtime and enhancing the user experience.

As organizations continue to migrate their workloads to the cloud, PaaS serves as a bridge between traditional on-premises infrastructure and the cloud-native world. PaaS platforms offer compatibility with various programming languages and frameworks, allowing developers to migrate and modernize their existing applications with ease. This compatibility ensures a smooth transition and minimizes disruption to ongoing business operations.

Moreover, PaaS supports the development of microservices-based architectures, a fundamental paradigm in modern software development. Microservices allow applications to be broken down into smaller, independently deployable components, promoting flexibility and scalability. PaaS platforms provide the necessary tools and services to build, deploy, and manage microservices, making them an ideal choice for organizations pursuing microservices-based strategies.

Looking ahead, the future of PaaS promises to be marked by continued innovation and adaptation to emerging technologies. Trends such as serverless computing, edge computing, and containerization are shaping the evolution of PaaS offerings. Serverless platforms abstract even more of the underlying infrastructure, enabling developers to focus solely on writing functions or code snippets that respond to specific events, further simplifying application development and reducing operational overhead.

Edge computing, on the other hand, extends the capabilities of PaaS to the edge of the network, enabling low-latency processing for IoT applications and real-time analytics. PaaS providers are increasingly investing in edge computing solutions to address the growing demand for edge services.

Containerization technologies, such as Docker and Kubernetes, are also becoming integral parts of PaaS platforms. These technologies enhance the portability and scalability of applications, making them well-suited for the dynamic nature of cloud environments. As PaaS providers integrate container orchestration and management capabilities, developers can take advantage of these tools to build and deploy containerized applications seamlessly.

In summary, Platform as a Service (PaaS) is a pivotal component of modern software development and cloud computing. It abstracts the underlying infrastructure, simplifying the development process, fostering collaboration, and enabling auto-scaling. PaaS platforms offer numerous advantages, including enhanced security, compliance, monitoring, and compatibility with diverse programming languages and frameworks. The future of PaaS holds exciting prospects, driven by trends like serverless computing, edge computing, and containerization, which promise to further streamline application development and deployment in the ever-evolving world of technology.

Platform as a Service (PaaS) is a transformative concept in the realm of cloud computing, offering a multitude of advantages for businesses and developers alike. It presents a comprehensive solution that simplifies the entire application development and deployment process. PaaS abstracts the complexities of infrastructure management, liberating developers from the burdens of server provisioning, hardware maintenance, and software updates. This abstraction allows developers to focus their energies on innovation, coding, and building applications that drive business value.

One of the primary advantages of PaaS is its ability to streamline the application development lifecycle. From the initial stages of conceptualization and coding to the testing, deployment, and ongoing management phases, PaaS offers a unified platform that encompasses all these critical aspects. This consolidation of tools, services, and resources within a single platform enhances collaboration and agility within development teams.

In contrast to Infrastructure as a Service (IaaS), where users are responsible for managing virtualized hardware resources, and Software as a Service (SaaS), where users consume pre-built software applications, PaaS occupies the middle ground. PaaS provides a development environment that empowers developers to create custom applications tailored to specific business requirements.

The core principle of PaaS revolves around abstracting the underlying infrastructure. By doing so, PaaS simplifies and streamlines various aspects of application development, including database management, server provisioning, and networking. Developers can leverage pre-built components, libraries, and services provided by the PaaS platform, significantly accelerating development cycles and enhancing overall productivity.

However, it's important to note that PaaS is not a one-size-fits-all solution. Instead, it caters to a wide range of applications, encompassing web and mobile apps, microservices, and IoT applications. The versatility of PaaS platforms allows developers to choose the tools and services that align with their specific project requirements. For instance, web application developers may utilize PaaS offerings for web hosting, databases, and content delivery, while data scientists may harness PaaS tools for big data analytics and machine learning.

To truly appreciate the advantages of PaaS, it's essential to understand how it fosters collaboration among development teams. PaaS provides a centralized environment for code sharing, version control, and collaborative development. This collaborative approach streamlines the development process, ensuring that multiple developers can work on a project simultaneously without conflicts or disruptions. Furthermore, PaaS platforms often integrate with popular development tools like Git and Jenkins, further enhancing team efficiency.

Another significant advantage of PaaS is its dynamic scaling capabilities. Applications hosted on PaaS platforms can auto-scale based on demand. This means that as user traffic and workload fluctuate, the application's capacity can automatically adjust to handle the changes. Developers can configure auto-scaling rules and policies, reducing the need for manual intervention and optimizing resource utilization.

PaaS platforms also contribute to the promotion of a DevOps culture within organizations. By blurring the lines between development and operations, PaaS empowers developers with more control over the deployment and management of their applications. This sense of ownership and accountability encourages collaboration between development and operations teams, resulting in faster deployment cycles and higher-quality applications.

Security and compliance are paramount considerations for businesses, and PaaS platforms have incorporated robust measures to address these concerns. Most PaaS providers offer built-in security features and compliance certifications, helping organizations meet regulatory requirements and protect sensitive data. These security measures encompass encryption, identity and access management, and threat detection, among others.

Furthermore, PaaS platforms provide comprehensive monitoring and analytics capabilities. Developers can gain real-time insights into their application's performance, enabling them to identify and address issues promptly. Monitoring dashboards, logs, and alerts facilitate proactive troubleshooting, reducing downtime and enhancing the user experience.

As organizations continue their migration to the cloud, PaaS serves as a bridge between traditional on-premises infrastructure and the cloud-native world. PaaS platforms offer compatibility with various programming languages and frameworks, facilitating the migration and modernization of existing applications. This compatibility ensures a smooth transition while minimizing disruption to ongoing business operations.

Moreover, PaaS platforms support the development of microservices-based architectures, a fundamental paradigm in modern software development. Microservices break down applications into smaller, independently deployable components, promoting flexibility and scalability. PaaS platforms provide the necessary tools and services to build, deploy, and manage microservices, making them an ideal choice for organizations pursuing microservices-based strategies.

Looking ahead, the future of PaaS holds promises of continued innovation and adaptation to emerging technologies. Trends such as serverless computing, edge computing, and containerization are shaping the evolution of PaaS offerings. Serverless platforms abstract even more of the underlying infrastructure, allowing developers to focus solely on writing functions or code snippets that respond to specific events, further simplifying application development and reducing operational overhead.

Edge computing extends the capabilities of PaaS to the edge of the network, enabling low-latency processing for IoT applications and real-time analytics. PaaS providers are increasingly investing in edge computing solutions to address the growing demand for edge services. Containerization technologies, such as Docker and Kubernetes, are also becoming integral parts of PaaS platforms. These technologies enhance the portability and scalability of applications, making them well-suited for the dynamic nature of cloud environments. As PaaS providers integrate container orchestration and management capabilities, developers can take advantage of these tools to build and deploy containerized applications seamlessly.

In summary, Platform as a Service (PaaS) offers a multitude of advantages, making it a transformative concept in cloud computing. PaaS simplifies the development process, enhances collaboration, supports auto-scaling, fosters a DevOps culture, and ensures security and compliance. Its compatibility with various programming languages and frameworks facilitates migration to the cloud, while its support for microservices-based architectures promotes flexibility and scalability. The future of PaaS is marked by ongoing innovation, driven by trends like serverless computing, edge computing, and containerization, which promise to further streamline application development and deployment in the ever-evolving world of technology.

Chapter 2: Getting Started with Azure Pipelines

Setting up Azure Pipelines is a crucial step in achieving streamlined and automated software development workflows. Azure Pipelines, a part of the Azure DevOps services suite, provides a robust and flexible platform for building, testing, and deploying applications across various environments. To begin the process, you need to have an Azure DevOps account and access to the Azure Portal. Once you have these prerequisites in place, you can start configuring and customizing your pipelines to meet your project's specific needs.

The first step in setting up Azure Pipelines is to create a new project within your Azure DevOps account. Projects serve as containers for your source code, build pipelines, and release pipelines, allowing you to organize your work efficiently. After creating a project, you can navigate to the "Pipelines" section within Azure DevOps to get started with creating your first pipeline.

Azure Pipelines offers two types of pipelines: build pipelines and release pipelines. Build pipelines are responsible for compiling your source code, running tests, and generating artifacts that can be deployed to various environments. Release pipelines, on the other hand, facilitate the deployment of these artifacts to target environments such as development, staging, and production.

To create a build pipeline, you'll need to define the source code repository where your application code *resides. Azure Pipelines supports various source code repositories, including Azure Repos, GitHub, Bitbucket, and others. Once you've connected your repository to Azure Pipelines, you can specify the branch or branches that should trigger the pipeline's execution whenever changes are pushed.*

Next, you'll need to configure the build tasks for your pipeline. Azure Pipelines provides a wide range of predefined tasks and templates that cater to common development scenarios. These tasks can include compiling code, running unit tests, packaging artifacts, and more. You can customize the sequence and configuration of these tasks to suit your project's requirements.

Azure Pipelines also supports the use of YAML-based configuration files, known as "pipeline as code." This approach allows you to define your build pipeline's configuration within a code file that can be version-controlled alongside your application code. YAML-based pipelines offer transparency and reproducibility, making it easier to manage complex build processes.

Once you've configured your build pipeline, you can trigger its execution manually or set up automated triggers based on code commits or pull requests. Automated triggers ensure that your code is built and tested automatically whenever changes are made, helping to catch and address issues early in the development process.

After successfully setting up your build pipeline, you can proceed to create release pipelines to deploy your application to different environments. Release pipelines define the stages and tasks required to deploy your application to target environments, ensuring consistency and reliability in your deployment process.

Each stage in a release pipeline represents an environment, such as development, testing, staging, or production. You can configure the deployment tasks and conditions for each stage to control when and how your application is deployed. Azure Pipelines provides deployment tasks for various platforms and technologies, including virtual machines, container orchestration platforms like Kubernetes, and serverless environments.

To ensure smooth deployments, you can also set up approvals and checks at each stage of your release pipeline. This allows designated stakeholders to review and approve deployments before they proceed to the next environment, adding an extra layer of control and security to your release process.

One of the advantages of using Azure Pipelines is its extensibility through integrations with third-party tools and services. You can enhance your pipelines by integrating them with external services for tasks such as code analysis, security scanning, and performance testing. These integrations can help you achieve a higher level of automation and quality assurance in your software development process.

Azure Pipelines also provides comprehensive monitoring and reporting capabilities. You can track the progress and status of your pipelines in real-time, enabling you to quickly identify and address any issues that may arise during the build and deployment processes. Detailed logs, build artifacts, and test results are readily accessible, aiding in troubleshooting and debugging.

In addition to monitoring, Azure Pipelines offers rich visualization tools and dashboards that provide insights into the health and performance of your pipelines. These tools help teams gain a better understanding of their development processes and identify areas for improvement.

Security is a top priority in any software development process, and Azure Pipelines offers robust security features. Access control, role-based permissions, and authentication mechanisms ensure that only authorized individuals can modify and execute pipelines. Additionally, Azure Pipelines supports secure storage of sensitive information, such as credentials and API keys, through secret variables and variable groups.

To facilitate collaboration among development teams, Azure Pipelines provides built-in integration with popular version control systems, including Git. This integration allows developers to work seamlessly within their preferred version control environment while leveraging the power of Azure Pipelines for continuous integration and continuous deployment (CI/CD).

As you configure and fine-tune your pipelines, it's essential to consider scalability and resource management. Azure Pipelines allows you to define agent pools and agent specifications to ensure that your pipelines have access to the necessary computing resources. You can also take advantage of Microsoft-hosted agents, which provide a scalable and managed *environment for running your build and deployment tasks.*

In summary, setting up Azure Pipelines is a fundamental step in achieving efficient and automated software development workflows. Azure Pipelines offers a flexible and extensible platform for building, testing, and deploying applications across various environments. By configuring build and release pipelines, integrating with external services, and leveraging monitoring and security features, development teams can streamline their processes, enhance collaboration, and deliver high-quality software products to their users. Creating your first pipeline in Azure Pipelines is an essential step toward achieving automation and efficiency in your software development process. To begin, you'll need to have an Azure DevOps account and access to the Azure Portal. Once you've fulfilled these prerequisites, you can dive into the process of configuring and customizing your pipeline to suit your project's unique needs. First and foremost, you'll want to navigate to the "Pipelines" section within your Azure DevOps project. This is where you'll initiate the creation of your first pipeline. Azure Pipelines offers two primary types of pipelines: build pipelines and release pipelines. Build pipelines are responsible for compiling your source code, running tests, and generating artifacts that can be deployed to various environments. Release pipelines, on the other hand, facilitate the deployment of these artifacts to your target environments.

When creating your pipeline, you'll be prompted to select a source code repository where your application code resides. Azure Pipelines supports a variety of source code repositories, including Azure Repos, GitHub, Bitbucket, and others. After connecting your repository to Azure Pipelines, you can specify the branch or branches that should trigger the pipeline's execution whenever code changes are pushed.

With your source code repository configured, you can proceed to define the build tasks for your pipeline. Azure Pipelines offers a wide range of predefined tasks and templates that cater to common development scenarios. These tasks can include compiling code, running unit tests, packaging artifacts, and more. The sequence and configuration of these tasks can be customized to align with your project's specific requirements.

An alternative approach to configuring your pipeline is to utilize YAML-based configuration files, often referred to as "pipeline as code." This method allows you to define your build pipeline's configuration within a code file that can be version-controlled alongside your application code. YAML-based pipelines offer transparency and reproducibility, making it easier to manage complex build processes.

Once you've configured your build pipeline, you can set up automated triggers based on code commits or pull requests. These triggers ensure that your code is built and tested automatically whenever changes are made, providing early feedback and helping to catch and address issues in the development process.

Successful creation of a build pipeline marks a significant milestone in automating your software development workflow. However, your journey doesn't *end there. The next logical step is to create release pipelines that facilitate the deployment of your application to different environments, such as development, testing, staging, and production.*

Release pipelines define the stages and tasks required to deploy your application to target environments. Each stage in a release pipeline represents an environment, and you can configure the deployment tasks and conditions for each stage to control when and how your application is deployed. Azure Pipelines provides deployment tasks for various platforms and technologies, including virtual machines, container orchestration platforms like Kubernetes, and serverless environments.

To ensure smooth deployments, you can set up approvals and checks at each stage of your release pipeline. This allows designated stakeholders to review and approve deployments before they proceed to the next environment, adding an extra layer of control and security to your release process. Azure Pipelines offers extensive integration capabilities, allowing you to enhance your pipelines by integrating them with third-party tools and services. These integrations can cover a wide range of tasks, including code analysis, security scanning, performance testing, and more. By leveraging these integrations, you can achieve a higher level of automation and quality assurance in your software development process.

In addition to automation, Azure Pipelines provides comprehensive monitoring and reporting capabilities. You can monitor the progress and status of your pipelines in real-time, enabling you to quickly identify and address any issues that may arise during the build and deployment processes. Detailed logs, build artifacts, and test results are readily accessible, aiding in troubleshooting and debugging.

Visual tools and dashboards offered by Azure Pipelines provide insights into the health and performance of your pipelines. These tools assist teams in gaining a better understanding of their development processes and identifying areas for improvement. Monitoring and visualization are essential components of a continuous improvement cycle, helping teams iterate and enhance their software development practices.

Security is a paramount concern in any software development process, and Azure Pipelines offers robust security features. Access control, role-based permissions, and authentication mechanisms ensure that only authorized individuals can modify and execute pipelines. Additionally, Azure Pipelines supports secure storage of sensitive information, such as credentials and API keys, through secret variables and variable groups.

Collaboration is a fundamental aspect of modern software development, and Azure Pipelines facilitates collaboration among development teams. Azure Pipelines provides built-in integration with popular version control systems, including Git. This integration allows developers to work seamlessly within their preferred version control environment while leveraging the power of Azure Pipelines for continuous integration and continuous deployment (CI/CD).

As you configure and fine-tune your pipelines, it's essential to consider scalability and resource management. Azure Pipelines allows you to define agent pools and agent specifications to ensure that your pipelines have access to the necessary computing resources. You can also take advantage of Microsoft-hosted agents, which provide a scalable and managed environment for running your build and deployment tasks.

In summary, creating your first pipeline in Azure Pipelines is a pivotal step toward achieving efficient and automated software development workflows. Azure Pipelines offers a flexible and extensible platform for building, testing, and deploying applications across various environments. By configuring build and release pipelines, integrating with external services, and leveraging monitoring and security features, development teams can streamline their processes, enhance collaboration, and deliver high-quality software products to their users.

Chapter 3: Understanding Google Cloud Platform (GCP)

An overview of Google Cloud Platform (GCP) reveals a powerful and comprehensive suite of cloud computing services designed to meet the diverse needs of businesses and developers. GCP is one of the leading cloud providers globally, offering a wide range of infrastructure and platform services, data analytics tools, machine learning capabilities, and more. At its core, GCP is built on the same infrastructure that powers Google's globally recognized products like Search, YouTube, and Gmail, providing reliability, scalability, and performance.

GCP encompasses a vast array of services organized into various categories, including Compute, Storage, Databases, Networking, Big Data, Machine Learning, Identity & Security, and more. These categories cater to different aspects of cloud computing, allowing users to leverage the services that best align with their project requirements.

One of the core components of GCP is its Compute services, which provide the foundational infrastructure for running virtual machines, containers, and applications. Google Compute Engine offers flexible virtual machine (VM) instances that can be tailored to suit specific workloads. Users can choose from various machine types, including standard, memory-optimized, and CPU-optimized instances, depending on their computational needs.

For container orchestration and management, GCP offers Google Kubernetes Engine (GKE), a managed Kubernetes service. GKE simplifies the deployment and scaling of containerized applications, making it easier for developers to manage container workloads effectively.

GCP's Storage services provide scalable and durable solutions for data storage. Google Cloud Storage offers a highly available and cost-effective object storage solution suitable for storing and serving a wide range of data, from multimedia files to backups. Google Cloud Filestore provides fully managed network-attached storage (NAS) for use with applications that require shared file systems.

When it comes to databases, GCP offers a variety of options to accommodate different use cases. Google Cloud SQL provides managed relational database services for popular database engines like MySQL, PostgreSQL, and SQL Server. For NoSQL databases, Google Cloud Firestore and Google Cloud Bigtable offer scalable and flexible solutions. Bigtable, in particular, is designed for handling large amounts of data with low latency, making it ideal for applications that require high-speed data access.

Networking is a critical aspect of cloud infrastructure, and GCP provides robust networking capabilities. Google Cloud Virtual Private Cloud (VPC) allows users to create isolated networks with customizable IP address ranges, subnets, and firewall rules. Google Cloud Load Balancing distributes traffic across multiple instances to ensure high availability and fault tolerance.

GCP's Big Data and Analytics services offer a wide range of tools for processing and analyzing data at scale. Google BigQuery, a fully managed data warehouse, enables users to run SQL-like queries on large datasets quickly. Dataflow, another GCP service, provides a unified stream and batch data processing model for real-time analytics and ETL (Extract, Transform, Load) workflows.

Machine Learning is a significant focus of GCP, with services like Google Cloud AI and Google Cloud AutoML allowing users to build and deploy machine learning models. TensorFlow, an open-source machine learning framework developed by Google, is also well-integrated into GCP's ecosystem, providing a powerful toolset for training and deploying machine learning models.

Identity and security are paramount in the cloud, and GCP offers robust identity management and security features. Google Cloud Identity and Access Management (IAM) allows organizations to control access to their resources and services securely. Google Cloud Identity provides a single sign-on (SSO) solution for managing user identities and access to applications.

Security features such as encryption at rest and in transit, security keys, and audit logs help protect data and maintain compliance with industry standards and regulations. GCP also offers Google Cloud Security Command Center, a centralized security management and data risk platform that provides insights into the security posture of your cloud resources.

GCP's DevOps and Development Tools support the entire software development lifecycle. Google Cloud Build automates the build and test processes, making it easier to manage continuous integration and continuous delivery (CI/CD) pipelines. Google Cloud Source Repositories provide Git repositories for version control, while Google Cloud Code offers an integrated development environment (IDE) for building, debugging, and deploying applications directly from the IDE.

GCP's ecosystem extends beyond its core services through an extensive marketplace of third-party solutions and partner offerings. This marketplace allows users to find and deploy pre-configured applications and services to enhance their cloud environment.

When it comes to hybrid and multi-cloud solutions, GCP provides options for connecting on-premises environments to the cloud. Google Cloud Anthos, a modern application platform, enables users to manage and deploy applications consistently across on-premises data centers and multiple cloud environments.

In summary, Google Cloud Platform (GCP) offers a comprehensive set of cloud computing services designed to meet the needs of businesses and developers. With a strong focus on compute, storage, databases, networking, big data, machine learning, identity and security, GCP provides a versatile and robust cloud infrastructure. Its rich ecosystem of tools, third-party solutions, and partner offerings allows users to build, deploy, and manage applications effectively. GCP's emphasis on security, scalability, and performance makes it a compelling choice for organizations seeking a cloud platform that can support their growth and innovation.

Key Platform as a Service (PaaS) services in Google Cloud Platform (GCP) encompass a diverse array of tools and capabilities that empower developers and organizations to build, deploy, and scale applications seamlessly. These services simplify the development process, reduce infrastructure management overhead, and accelerate time-to-market for new applications.

Google App Engine is a fully managed PaaS offering that allows developers to build and deploy web applications and APIs without worrying about the underlying infrastructure. It supports multiple programming languages, including Python, Java, Node.js, and Go, making it accessible to a broad range of developers.

Google Cloud Functions provides a serverless computing environment for executing event-driven functions. Developers can write code to respond to various triggers, such as HTTP requests, cloud storage changes, and database updates. Google Cloud Functions automatically scales resources to handle the workload, ensuring cost efficiency and reliability.

Cloud Run is a container-based PaaS service that enables developers to deploy and manage containerized applications easily. It abstracts away infrastructure concerns, allowing developers to focus solely on building and deploying containerized applications using Docker containers.

Google Cloud Composer offers managed Apache Airflow for orchestrating workflows and data pipelines. It simplifies the task of scheduling, monitoring, and managing complex data processing tasks and provides a visual interface for designing and monitoring workflows.

Firebase is a comprehensive mobile and web application development platform that offers a range of PaaS services. It includes tools for real-time database management, authentication, hosting, and cloud functions, making it an excellent choice for building mobile and web applications quickly.

Google Cloud Dataflow is a fully managed stream and batch data processing service. It allows developers to design, deploy, and execute data pipelines for real-time analytics and data transformation tasks. Dataflow is built on Apache Beam and supports multiple programming languages.

Google Cloud Spanner is a globally distributed and horizontally scalable relational database service. It combines the benefits of traditional relational databases with the scalability and high availability of NoSQL databases. Spanner is ideal for building globally distributed applications that require strong consistency and high performance.

Google Cloud SQL offers managed database services for popular relational database engines, including MySQL, PostgreSQL, and SQL Server. It simplifies database management tasks, such as replication, backups, and scaling, allowing developers to focus on application development.

Cloud Bigtable is a highly scalable, NoSQL database service designed for massive workloads and real-time analytics. It is well-suited for applications that require high-throughput and low-latency access to large datasets, such as IoT and time-series data analysis.

Google Cloud Memorystore provides a managed in-memory data store service that is compatible with the Redis open-source in-memory database. It offers low-latency data access for caching and real-time applications, helping developers improve application performance.

Google Cloud Pub/Sub is a messaging service that enables asynchronous communication between components of distributed applications. It supports event-driven architectures and decouples the communication between different services, enhancing scalability and reliability.

Google Cloud Endpoints simplifies the development of APIs by generating server and client code automatically. It provides tools for managing and securing APIs, making it easier for developers to expose their applications' functionality as RESTful APIs.

Apigee, now part of Google Cloud, offers a comprehensive API management platform that enables organizations to design, secure, and analyze APIs. It provides features for API traffic management, security, and analytics, allowing organizations to create robust API ecosystems.

Google Cloud IoT Core is a managed service for building and managing IoT (Internet of Things) applications. It provides capabilities for securely connecting, managing, and ingesting data from IoT devices, making it easier to build scalable and secure IoT solutions.

Google Cloud Machine Learning Engine offers a managed environment for training and deploying machine learning models. It supports popular machine learning frameworks like TensorFlow and scikit-learn, allowing data scientists and developers to build and deploy models at scale.

Google Cloud AutoML is a suite of machine learning services that enables developers to build custom machine learning models without extensive expertise in machine learning. It includes services for vision, natural language, and tabular data, making machine learning more accessible.

Google Cloud Vision AI and Google Cloud Natural Language AI are pre-trained machine learning APIs that provide capabilities for image recognition and natural language processing, respectively. These APIs allow developers to integrate powerful AI capabilities into their applications with ease.

Google Cloud Speech-to-Text and Google Cloud Text-to-Speech are machine learning APIs that enable developers to incorporate speech recognition and text-to-speech synthesis into their applications. They are useful for building voice-enabled applications and services.

Google Cloud Translation API offers language translation capabilities, allowing developers to build multilingual applications. It supports translation between multiple languages and can be used for text and website translation.

These key PaaS services in GCP collectively form a robust and versatile ecosystem that supports a wide range of application development and data processing needs. Whether you are building web applications, deploying machine learning models, managing databases, or processing real-time data streams, GCP's PaaS offerings provide the tools and services to simplify development, reduce operational complexity, and accelerate innovation.

Chapter 4: Mastering Microsoft Azure PaaS Offerings

Exploring Azure Platform as a Service (PaaS) solutions opens the door to a world of cloud-based services and tools designed to simplify application development and deployment. Azure PaaS provides a wide range of services that enable developers to focus on writing code and building applications without the overhead of managing infrastructure.

Azure App Service is a central piece of Azure PaaS, offering a fully managed platform for building, deploying, and scaling web applications. It supports various programming languages, including .NET, Java, Python, Node.js, and PHP, making it accessible to a diverse community of developers.

Azure Functions takes serverless computing to the next level, allowing developers to write code that responds to events and triggers without the need to manage servers. It's ideal for building event-driven applications and microservices.

Azure Logic Apps provide a way to automate workflows and integrate applications and services. Using a visual designer, developers can create workflows that connect various Azure services and external systems, streamlining business processes.

Azure Kubernetes Service (AKS) simplifies the management of containerized applications using Kubernetes. It provides a managed Kubernetes cluster, making it easier to deploy, scale, and orchestrate containers.

Azure Cosmos DB is a globally distributed, multi-model database service that offers high availability, low-latency access, and scalability. It supports NoSQL data models, including document, key-value, graph, and column-family, making it suitable for a wide range of applications.

Azure SQL Database provides a fully managed relational database service that supports SQL Server. It offers high availability, automatic backups, and built-in intelligence features for optimizing performance.

Azure Functions is a serverless compute service that enables developers to build and run event-driven applications without the need to manage infrastructure. It allows you to write code in response to events and triggers, making it well-suited for scenarios like microservices, IoT, and serverless APIs.

Azure Event Grid is a fully managed event routing service that simplifies event-driven architectures. It allows you to react to events from Azure services, custom applications, and external sources, enabling real-time event processing.

Azure Service Fabric is a distributed systems platform that simplifies building and managing microservices-based applications. It provides tools for deploying, managing, and scaling microservices and stateful services.

Azure Functions is a serverless compute service that enables developers to write code in response to events and triggers without managing infrastructure. It supports multiple programming languages, making it versatile for a wide range of applications.

Azure DevOps Services, formerly known as Visual Studio Team Services (VSTS), provides a set of development and collaboration tools for building and releasing software. It includes features for version control, build automation, release management, and application monitoring.

Azure Active Directory (Azure AD) is Microsoft's identity and access management service for authenticating and authorizing users and applications. It provides single sign-on (SSO) capabilities and supports integration with on-premises directories.

Azure Functions is a serverless compute service that enables developers to build and deploy event-driven functions. It automatically scales to handle incoming requests, making it suitable for building serverless APIs and backend services.

Azure Container Instances offer a way to run containers in the cloud without managing virtual machines. It provides a quick and straightforward way to deploy containers for tasks like batch processing and running background jobs.

Azure PaaS solutions are designed to simplify application development and deployment by abstracting away the complexities of infrastructure management. They provide a range of services and tools that cater to various development scenarios, allowing developers to choose the right tools for their projects.

Azure PaaS solutions support a variety of programming languages and frameworks, making them accessible to developers with different skill sets and preferences. Whether you are building web applications, APIs, microservices, or data processing pipelines, there is an Azure PaaS service to meet your needs.

One of the key advantages of Azure PaaS is the ability to scale applications easily. Azure App Service, Azure Functions, and Azure Kubernetes Service all offer automatic scaling capabilities, ensuring that your applications can handle varying levels of traffic without manual intervention.

Azure PaaS solutions also integrate seamlessly with other Azure services, allowing you to build end-to-end solutions that encompass everything from data storage and analytics to machine learning and artificial intelligence.

Azure Logic Apps provide a visual designer that simplifies the creation of workflows and integrations between different systems and services. This makes it easier to automate business processes and connect applications.

Azure PaaS solutions are designed with security in mind, offering features such as identity and access management, encryption, and threat detection. Azure Active Directory (Azure AD) provides robust authentication and authorization capabilities for applications and users.

Azure PaaS solutions also support DevOps practices, enabling teams to automate build and release pipelines, monitor application performance, and gain insights into usage patterns.

Azure PaaS solutions are available in multiple regions worldwide, allowing you to deploy applications close to your users for low-latency access and high availability.

Azure PaaS solutions provide a wide range of developer tools and SDKs, making it easy to integrate Azure services into your development workflow. Whether you are using Visual Studio, Visual Studio Code, or other popular development environments, you can leverage Azure PaaS services effectively.

Azure PaaS solutions are backed by Microsoft's extensive network of data centers and global presence, ensuring reliable and scalable performance for your applications.

In summary, exploring Azure PaaS solutions reveals a wealth of tools and services that simplify application development and deployment. From web applications and serverless computing to container orchestration and database management, Azure PaaS offers a diverse set of solutions to meet your development needs. Whether you are a developer, IT professional, or data scientist, Azure PaaS provides the tools and services to help you build, deploy, and scale applications with ease.

Practical use cases for Azure Platform as a Service (PaaS) solutions span a wide range of industries and application scenarios, showcasing the versatility and utility of these cloud-based services. One prominent use case is web application development, where Azure App Service offers a fully managed platform for building and deploying web applications with ease. Developers can leverage various programming languages and *frameworks to create responsive and scalable web apps, whether it's an e-commerce site, a content management system, or a customer portal.*

In the realm of e-commerce, Azure PaaS solutions find practical application in online retail platforms. Azure SQL Database, for example, provides a robust and scalable backend database for managing product catalogs, customer information, and transaction data. Azure Functions can be used to handle order processing, inventory management, and real-time pricing updates, ensuring a seamless shopping experience for customers. For organizations in the healthcare sector, Azure PaaS solutions play a critical role in managing electronic health records (EHRs) and healthcare applications. Azure Cosmos DB, with its globally distributed and highly available database service, can securely store and manage patient data while complying with stringent healthcare data privacy regulations. Azure Logic Apps can automate workflows for appointment scheduling, patient registration, and billing, streamlining administrative tasks. The financial industry benefits from Azure PaaS solutions in various ways, such as fraud detection and financial analytics. Azure Machine Learning allows financial institutions to build predictive models for identifying fraudulent transactions, while Azure Databricks facilitates data analysis and reporting for risk assessment and investment strategies.

Media and entertainment companies leverage Azure PaaS solutions for content delivery and media processing. Azure Content Delivery Network (CDN) ensures low-latency and high-performance content delivery to global audiences, enhancing the streaming experience for video-on-demand platforms and live streaming events. Azure Media Services can be used to encode, package, and distribute media content efficiently.

Manufacturing and supply chain management rely on Azure PaaS solutions to optimize operations and enhance productivity. Azure IoT Hub enables the connection and management of IoT devices, facilitating real-time monitoring of equipment, predictive maintenance, and inventory tracking. Azure Stream Analytics processes sensor data to identify production bottlenecks and supply chain inefficiencies, leading to informed decision-making.

Government agencies leverage Azure PaaS solutions for digital transformation and citizen services. Azure Government provides a dedicated cloud environment with compliance certifications for government-specific requirements. Azure Cognitive Services can be used to develop applications that enhance accessibility, such as speech recognition and language translation tools for government websites.

Education institutions utilize Azure PaaS solutions to enhance learning experiences and administrative processes. Azure DevTest Labs offers a cost-effective environment for creating development and testing environments for educational software and applications. Azure Active Directory simplifies identity management and access control for students and staff, ensuring secure access to resources.

For startups and small businesses, Azure PaaS solutions provide a cost-effective and scalable platform for launching innovative products and services. Azure Kubernetes Service (AKS) enables startups to containerize their applications and manage them efficiently, while Azure Functions and Logic Apps simplify the development of serverless applications.

In the field of gaming, Azure PaaS solutions power online gaming platforms and multiplayer experiences. Azure Virtual Machines offer scalable game server hosting, ensuring low-latency gameplay for players worldwide. Azure PlayFab provides tools for game analytics, player engagement, and live game operations.

Retailers and e-commerce platforms utilize Azure PaaS solutions for customer relationship management (CRM) and personalized marketing. Azure Cosmos DB can store customer profiles and purchase history, allowing retailers to deliver personalized product recommendations. Azure Logic Apps automate marketing campaigns, email notifications, and customer support processes.

The energy sector leverages Azure PaaS solutions for managing renewable energy resources and optimizing energy grids. Azure IoT solutions monitor wind turbines, solar panels, and energy consumption patterns, enabling efficient energy production and distribution. Azure Stream Analytics processes real-time data from smart meters to detect anomalies and improve energy grid stability.

In the travel and hospitality industry, Azure PaaS solutions enhance customer experiences and streamline operations. Azure Cognitive Services can provide language translation services for international travelers, while Azure Machine Learning models can predict hotel room availability and pricing based on historical data and market trends.

Non-profit organizations benefit from Azure PaaS solutions for fundraising, donor management, and program delivery. Azure Functions can automate donor communication and event registration, while Azure SQL Database can store donor information securely. Azure Logic Apps facilitate the automation of administrative tasks, allowing non-profits to focus on their missions.

These practical use cases highlight the diverse applications of Azure PaaS solutions across industries. Whether it's improving healthcare services, optimizing supply chains, enhancing education, or delivering innovative products, Azure PaaS empowers organizations to leverage cloud-based services to achieve their goals efficiently and effectively.

Chapter 5: Exploring IBM Cloud PaaS Solutions

An overview of IBM Cloud Platform as a Service (PaaS) reveals a robust set of cloud-based services designed to support application development, deployment, and management. IBM Cloud PaaS offers a comprehensive suite of tools and solutions tailored to meet the diverse needs of developers and organizations across various industries. It is built on a foundation of reliability, scalability, and security, making it a compelling choice for businesses seeking cloud-based solutions.

IBM Cloud Foundry provides a core platform for application deployment and scaling. It simplifies the process of building, deploying, and managing applications by abstracting away the underlying infrastructure. Developers can focus on writing code and defining application logic while IBM Cloud Foundry takes care of the operational aspects, such as provisioning and scaling resources.

One of the key benefits of IBM Cloud PaaS is its support for multiple programming languages and frameworks. Whether you are developing applications in Java, Node.js, Python, Ruby, or other languages, IBM Cloud PaaS offers a compatible runtime environment. This versatility allows developers to choose the tools and languages they are most comfortable with, promoting productivity and flexibility.

IBM Cloud Kubernetes Service (IKS) is a managed Kubernetes service that simplifies container *orchestration and management. It provides a highly available and scalable Kubernetes cluster, making it easier for organizations to deploy and manage containerized applications. With IKS, developers can take advantage of the benefits of containers while reducing the operational overhead.*

IBM Cloud Databases offer managed database services that cater to various data storage needs. Whether you require a relational database with IBM Db2, a NoSQL database with IBM Cloudant, or a fully managed PostgreSQL database, IBM Cloud Databases provide options for different use cases. These services alleviate the complexities of database administration, including backup, scaling, and high availability.

For organizations focused on artificial intelligence (AI) and machine learning (ML), IBM Cloud PaaS offers Watson Studio, a comprehensive platform for data scientists and developers. Watson Studio simplifies the process of building, training, and deploying machine learning models. It provides tools for data preparation, model development, and model deployment, making AI and ML accessible to a broader audience.

IBM Cloud Functions is a serverless computing platform that enables developers to write and deploy event-driven functions without managing servers. It supports event triggers from various sources, including HTTP requests, message queues, and databases. Developers can use IBM Cloud Functions to build scalable and responsive applications that automatically react to events.

IBM Cloud Continuous Delivery provides tools and services for automating the software development lifecycle. It includes capabilities for continuous integration, continuous delivery, and DevOps practices. Developers can automate build and deployment pipelines, facilitating the rapid and reliable delivery of software updates.

Security is a top priority in IBM Cloud PaaS. It offers a range of security features, including identity and access management, encryption, and threat detection. IBM Cloud Identity and Access Management (IAM) allows organizations to control access to their resources and services securely. Data encryption at rest and in transit helps protect sensitive information, ensuring compliance with industry standards and regulations.

IBM Cloud Monitoring and Observability tools provide insights into the performance and health of applications and services. Developers and operators can monitor application logs, metrics, and traces to identify issues and optimize performance. This visibility into the application environment aids in troubleshooting and maintaining application reliability.

IBM Cloud Integration offers tools and services for connecting applications, data, and services. It supports hybrid cloud and multi-cloud scenarios, allowing organizations to integrate on-premises systems with cloud-based solutions. IBM App Connect simplifies the creation of integration flows and enables data synchronization across different systems.

IBM Cloud PaaS is designed with enterprise-grade reliability in mind. It provides high availability and disaster recovery options to ensure business continuity. Organizations can deploy their applications across multiple IBM Cloud regions for redundancy and failover capabilities.

IBM Cloud Private is an on-premises cloud platform that extends the benefits of IBM Cloud PaaS to private data centers. It enables organizations to build and manage cloud-native applications on their infrastructure while maintaining control and security. IBM Cloud Private supports containerized applications and Kubernetes orchestration, fostering consistency between on-premises and cloud environments.

In summary, the IBM Cloud PaaS overview highlights a comprehensive set of cloud-based services and tools tailored to support application development and deployment. With a focus on versatility, security, and reliability, IBM Cloud PaaS offers solutions for a wide range of development scenarios, from container orchestration to AI and ML. Developers and organizations can leverage these services to accelerate innovation and streamline application development processes while ensuring data security and compliance.

Use cases and benefits of IBM Cloud Platform as a Service (PaaS) are diverse and encompass various industries and application scenarios, showcasing the value and versatility of this cloud-based offering. One prominent use case is application modernization, where organizations leverage IBM Cloud PaaS to migrate and modernize legacy applications, reducing technical debt and improving agility.

In the healthcare sector, IBM Cloud PaaS supports telemedicine applications, enabling healthcare providers to deliver remote consultations and monitor patients' health in real time. These applications enhance access to healthcare services, particularly for patients in remote or underserved areas.

For financial institutions, IBM Cloud PaaS offers solutions for regulatory compliance and risk management. IBM Cloud Databases provide secure and scalable data storage for sensitive financial data, while Watson Studio helps develop machine learning models for fraud detection and credit risk assessment.

Manufacturing companies benefit from IBM Cloud PaaS for optimizing supply chain operations. IBM Cloud Private allows manufacturers to build and deploy cloud-native applications for demand forecasting, inventory management, and production optimization. These applications enhance efficiency and reduce costs.

In the retail industry, IBM Cloud PaaS supports personalized marketing and customer engagement. IBM Cloud Functions enable retailers to develop serverless applications for real-time product recommendations, personalized promotions, and customer feedback analysis. These capabilities enhance the shopping experience and increase customer loyalty.

The energy sector leverages IBM Cloud PaaS for smart grid management and renewable energy integration. IBM Cloud IoT solutions connect and monitor energy infrastructure, enabling real-time data analysis for efficient energy distribution and consumption. This results in reduced energy costs and environmental benefits.

For educational institutions, IBM Cloud PaaS facilitates online learning and student services. IBM Cloud Video Streaming allows educators to deliver virtual lectures and interactive content, while IBM Cloud Databases securely store student records and academic data.

Government agencies utilize IBM Cloud PaaS for citizen services and data analytics. IBM Cloud Private provides a secure environment for developing and deploying applications that streamline government operations and enhance citizen engagement. IBM Watson enables natural language processing and sentiment analysis for public opinion monitoring.

Startups and small businesses benefit from IBM Cloud PaaS for rapid application development and scaling. IBM Cloud Functions and IBM Cloud Foundry offer cost-effective options for developing and deploying applications without the need for extensive infrastructure management.

In the gaming industry, IBM Cloud PaaS powers multiplayer gaming experiences and in-game analytics. IBM Cloud Kubernetes Service (IKS) provides scalable game server hosting, ensuring low-latency gameplay for players worldwide. IBM Cloud Databases support leaderboards and player profiles.

Non-profit organizations leverage IBM Cloud PaaS for fundraising and donor management. IBM Cloud Functions automate donor communication and event registration, while IBM Cloud Databases store donor information securely. IBM Cloud PaaS allows non-profits *to focus on their missions while efficiently managing administrative tasks.*

The automotive sector utilizes IBM Cloud PaaS for connected car applications and vehicle data analytics. IBM Cloud IoT solutions enable automakers to collect and analyze vehicle sensor data, leading to predictive maintenance and improved vehicle performance.

In the travel and hospitality industry, IBM Cloud PaaS enhances customer experiences and operational efficiency. IBM Cloud Private provides a platform for developing and deploying cloud-native applications for booking and reservation systems. IBM Watson enables multilingual customer support and chatbots for seamless communication.

Non-governmental organizations (NGOs) leverage IBM Cloud PaaS for disaster response and humanitarian efforts. IBM Cloud Functions support real-time data processing for disaster monitoring, while IBM Cloud Databases store critical information for relief efforts.

These use cases highlight the practical applications of IBM Cloud PaaS across various industries and scenarios. Whether it's enhancing healthcare accessibility, optimizing supply chains, improving educational services, or enabling innovative startups, IBM Cloud PaaS provides the tools and services to address a wide range of challenges and opportunities.

The benefits of IBM Cloud PaaS extend beyond specific use cases, encompassing advantages such as scalability, agility, cost-effectiveness, and security. Organizations can scale their applications and infrastructure according to demand, ensuring optimal performance and resource utilization. This scalability allows businesses to accommodate growth and respond to changing market conditions effectively.

The agility provided by IBM Cloud PaaS enables rapid application development and deployment. Developers can leverage pre-built services and development frameworks to accelerate the development lifecycle, reducing time-to-market for new products and features. This agility is particularly valuable in fast-paced industries and competitive markets.

Cost-effectiveness is a significant benefit of IBM Cloud PaaS. Organizations can leverage a pay-as-you-go pricing model, minimizing upfront capital expenses and optimizing operational costs. This cost structure allows businesses to align their IT spending with actual usage, resulting in cost savings and improved financial flexibility.

Security is a paramount consideration in IBM Cloud PaaS. IBM Cloud Identity and Access Management (IAM) provides robust identity and access control, ensuring that only authorized users and applications can access resources. Encryption and threat detection features enhance data protection and compliance with regulatory requirements.

Furthermore, the managed services offered by IBM Cloud PaaS alleviate the operational burden on organizations. With managed databases, serverless computing, and container orchestration, businesses can focus on application development and innovation while IBM Cloud takes care of infrastructure management, maintenance, and security.

In summary, IBM Cloud PaaS serves as a versatile and valuable solution for organizations across various industries and use cases. Whether it's modernizing legacy applications, enhancing customer experiences, optimizing operations, or supporting innovative initiatives, IBM Cloud PaaS offers the tools, flexibility, and benefits to meet the demands of a dynamic and competitive digital landscape.

Chapter 6: Best Practices for PaaS Deployment

Effective Platform as a Service (PaaS) deployment is crucial for organizations seeking to harness the full potential of cloud computing. Successful PaaS deployment strategies require careful planning, consideration of business goals, and alignment with technical requirements. One fundamental strategy is to start with a clear understanding of your organization's objectives, as this will guide all subsequent decisions and actions.

Begin by defining your specific business needs and objectives for PaaS deployment. Consider factors such as application scalability, agility, cost savings, and time-to-market. Having a well-defined purpose for adopting PaaS will help you make informed decisions throughout the deployment process.

Selecting the right PaaS provider is a critical step in the deployment strategy. Evaluate providers based on factors like service offerings, compliance with industry standards, geographic presence, and support for the programming languages and frameworks your organization uses. Assessing the provider's reliability, security measures, and performance is essential to ensure a successful deployment.

Consider the compatibility of your existing applications and infrastructure with the chosen PaaS platform. A well-thought-out strategy includes evaluating whether your current applications can be migrated or adapted to run effectively in the PaaS environment. Compatibility assessments help identify potential challenges and inform the migration plan.

Develop a migration plan that outlines the steps and timeline for moving your applications to the PaaS environment. This plan should include thorough testing and validation procedures to ensure that applications perform as expected in the new platform. A phased approach to migration can reduce risks and disruptions to ongoing operations.

Address data management and integration in your deployment strategy. Plan for data migration, storage, and backup strategies in the PaaS environment. Ensure that data integration with other systems and services is seamless and reliable to avoid data silos and operational inefficiencies.

Implement robust security measures as part of your deployment strategy. PaaS providers typically offer security features, but it's essential to configure and manage them effectively to protect your applications and data. Consider encryption, access control, authentication, and regular security audits as integral components of your PaaS deployment.

Focus on continuous monitoring and performance optimization in your deployment strategy. Implement tools and processes for monitoring application health, performance metrics, and resource utilization. Proactively address any bottlenecks or issues to ensure optimal application performance.

Establish clear governance and compliance policies as part of your deployment strategy. Define roles and responsibilities for managing and maintaining the PaaS environment. Ensure compliance with industry regulations and internal policies related to data privacy, security, and governance.

Encourage collaboration and communication among teams involved in PaaS deployment. Effective cross-functional coordination between development, operations, and security teams is essential for a successful deployment. Foster a culture of collaboration to streamline workflows and address challenges promptly.

Consider the scalability requirements of your applications in the PaaS environment. Ensure that your deployment strategy accounts for both vertical and horizontal scaling to accommodate fluctuations in traffic and demand. Scalability is a key benefit of PaaS and should be leveraged effectively.

Implement a robust backup and disaster recovery strategy as part of your deployment plan. Regularly back up critical data and configurations, and establish procedures for rapid recovery in the event of data loss or system failures. A well-prepared disaster recovery plan helps minimize downtime and data loss.

Invest in training and skill development for your team members as part of your PaaS deployment strategy. Ensure that your staff is equipped with the knowledge and skills needed to effectively manage and operate within the PaaS environment. Training and upskilling initiatives are essential for long-term success.

Stay informed about updates, enhancements, and new features offered by your PaaS provider. Regularly assess whether new capabilities can benefit your applications and operations. Embrace a culture of continuous improvement and adapt your deployment strategy accordingly.

Regularly review and refine your PaaS deployment strategy to align with evolving business goals and technological advancements. Monitor the performance of your applications in the PaaS environment and gather feedback from users to identify areas for improvement and optimization.

In summary, effective PaaS deployment strategies require a holistic approach that encompasses business goals, technical considerations, security measures, and ongoing optimization efforts. By carefully planning and executing your PaaS deployment strategy, you can leverage the benefits of cloud computing to drive innovation, efficiency, and competitiveness within your organization. Seamless Platform as a Service (PaaS) implementation is a critical endeavor for organizations looking to harness the power of cloud computing effectively. Implementing PaaS solutions requires careful planning, attention to detail, and a focus on key considerations to ensure a smooth transition to the cloud. Here are some valuable tips to guide you toward a seamless PaaS implementation.

Define Clear Objectives: Start by defining clear objectives for your PaaS implementation. Understand the specific business goals and outcomes you aim to achieve with PaaS, such as increased agility, reduced costs, or improved scalability.

Select the Right PaaS Provider: Carefully evaluate PaaS providers based on their offerings, support for your technology stack, compliance with industry standards, and reputation for reliability. Choose a provider that aligns with your organization's needs and goals.

Assess Application Compatibility: Assess the compatibility of your existing applications with the chosen PaaS platform. Determine whether any modifications or reconfiguration will be necessary to ensure a seamless transition to the cloud.

Develop a Comprehensive Migration Plan: Create a detailed migration plan that outlines the steps, timelines, and dependencies for moving your applications and data to the PaaS environment. Consider a phased approach to minimize disruptions.

Test Thoroughly: Prioritize testing throughout the migration process. Rigorously test applications in the PaaS environment to identify and address any issues related to performance, security, and functionality.

Optimize Performance: Implement performance monitoring and optimization tools to ensure that your applications run efficiently in the PaaS environment. Continuously monitor key performance indicators and make necessary adjustments.

Focus on Security: Security should be a top priority. Configure security settings, access controls, and encryption to protect your applications and data in the PaaS environment. Stay vigilant for security threats and vulnerabilities.

Implement Automation: Leverage automation tools and scripts to streamline deployment, scaling, and management processes. Automation reduces manual intervention, minimizes errors, and enhances efficiency.

Establish Governance Policies: Define governance policies and best practices for managing resources, access control, and compliance within the PaaS environment. Ensure that your organization adheres to these policies.

Encourage Collaboration: Foster collaboration and communication among teams involved in PaaS implementation, including development, operations, and security. Effective cross-functional collaboration enhances decision-making and problem-solving.

Scale Appropriately: Consider scalability requirements for your applications. Ensure that your PaaS implementation can scale horizontally and vertically to accommodate changes in traffic and demand.

Back Up and Disaster Recovery: Develop a robust backup and disaster recovery strategy. Regularly back up critical data and configurations, and establish procedures for rapid recovery in case of unexpected events.

Invest in Training: Invest in training and skill development for your team members. Equip your staff with the knowledge and expertise needed to effectively manage and operate within the PaaS environment.

Stay Informed: Stay informed about updates and new features offered by your PaaS provider. Regularly assess whether new capabilities can benefit your applications and operations.

Review and Iterate: Conduct regular reviews of your PaaS implementation to identify areas for improvement and optimization. Gather feedback from users and stakeholders to refine your approach.

Budget Wisely: Manage your budget effectively by monitoring PaaS-related costs and optimizing resource utilization. Ensure that your spending aligns with your organization's financial goals.

Compliance and Regulation: Stay compliant with industry regulations and data privacy standards relevant to your business. Regularly review and update your compliance measures to meet evolving requirements.

Document Everything: Maintain comprehensive documentation of your PaaS implementation, including configurations, security settings, and operational procedures. Documentation helps with troubleshooting and knowledge sharing.

Plan for Future Growth: Consider the long-term scalability and flexibility of your PaaS implementation. Ensure that it can accommodate future growth and evolving business needs.

Continuous Improvement: Embrace a culture of continuous improvement. Continuously assess the performance and efficiency of your PaaS implementation and adapt your strategies accordingly.

In summary, seamless PaaS implementation requires a strategic approach that encompasses planning, testing, security, collaboration, and ongoing optimization. By following these tips and best practices, organizations can navigate the complexities of PaaS adoption and reap the benefits of cloud computing while minimizing disruptions and maximizing success.

Chapter 7: Integrating DevOps into PaaS Environments

The role of DevOps in Platform as a Service (PaaS) is pivotal, as it plays a significant part in enabling organizations to maximize the benefits of cloud-based application development and deployment. DevOps, a cultural and collaborative approach that emphasizes communication, integration, and automation between development and IT operations teams, becomes even more critical in the context of PaaS.

DevOps in PaaS fosters a culture of collaboration and teamwork where developers and operations professionals work closely together to streamline the application development and deployment lifecycle. This collaboration begins with the early stages of application design and extends throughout the entire application's lifecycle.

One of the primary roles of DevOps in PaaS is to facilitate continuous integration and continuous delivery (CI/CD) pipelines. DevOps teams design, implement, and manage CI/CD pipelines that automate the building, testing, and deployment of applications in the PaaS environment. These pipelines ensure that code changes can be rapidly and reliably delivered to production, reducing the time-to-market for new features and improvements.

DevOps also focuses on infrastructure as code (IaC) within PaaS environments. Infrastructure as code allows infrastructure provisioning, configuration, and *management to be treated as code, enabling teams to automate infrastructure tasks and ensure consistency across environments. This approach aligns well with the self-service provisioning capabilities offered by PaaS platforms, allowing DevOps teams to provision the necessary resources efficiently.*

In addition to automation, DevOps emphasizes monitoring and observability in PaaS environments. DevOps teams implement monitoring solutions that track application performance, resource utilization, and other key metrics in real-time. These insights enable proactive issue detection and resolution, enhancing the reliability and availability of applications.

DevOps practices also play a role in ensuring the security of PaaS-based applications. Security considerations are integrated into the CI/CD pipelines, with automated security testing and vulnerability scanning being part of the development and deployment process. This proactive approach helps identify and address security issues early in the development cycle.

Another essential aspect of DevOps in PaaS is the management of configurations and environment consistency. DevOps teams use tools and practices to maintain consistency across development, testing, staging, and production environments. This ensures that applications behave consistently across different stages of the deployment pipeline.

DevOps in PaaS environments embraces the concept of microservices and containerization. DevOps teams leverage container orchestration platforms like Kubernetes to manage containerized applications efficiently. This approach allows applications to be broken down into smaller, manageable components that can be developed, tested, and deployed independently.

Collaboration between development and operations extends to incident management and response. DevOps teams establish incident response procedures that involve both development and operations personnel. This collaborative approach accelerates issue resolution and minimizes downtime.

DevOps in PaaS also promotes a culture of continuous improvement. DevOps teams regularly conduct post-incident reviews, retrospectives, and performance evaluations to identify areas for enhancement. This iterative process drives ongoing optimization and refinement of the development and deployment practices.

Furthermore, DevOps in PaaS embraces the concept of infrastructure as a service (IaaS) abstraction. PaaS platforms abstract the underlying infrastructure, allowing DevOps teams to focus on application development and deployment without the need to manage servers and hardware. This abstraction simplifies infrastructure management and accelerates application delivery.

DevOps practices in PaaS environments align with the principles of scalability and elasticity. DevOps teams design applications to be scalable, capable of handling increased workloads efficiently. They leverage the auto-scaling capabilities of PaaS platforms to automatically adjust resources based on demand.

Collaboration and communication are key tenets of DevOps in PaaS. DevOps teams use collaboration tools, chat platforms, and shared documentation to ensure that development and operations personnel are in sync and have visibility into each other's work. Effective communication enhances transparency and accelerates issue resolution.

In summary, the role of DevOps in Platform as a Service is multifaceted and integral to achieving the full potential of cloud-based application development and deployment. DevOps practices foster collaboration, automation, monitoring, security, and continuous improvement in PaaS environments. By embracing DevOps principles and methodologies, organizations can streamline their application development processes, enhance the reliability of their applications, and accelerate their digital transformation efforts in PaaS. DevOps tools play a critical role in the integration of Platform as a Service (PaaS) solutions into the software development and deployment pipeline. These tools are designed to automate and streamline various aspects of the development, testing, and deployment processes within a PaaS environment. One of the essential categories of DevOps tools for PaaS integration is continuous integration (CI) and continuous delivery (CD) tools. CI/CD tools, such as Jenkins, Travis CI, and CircleCI, enable developers to automate the building, testing, and deployment of applications in a PaaS environment. They help maintain consistency and reliability in the development pipeline by automating repetitive tasks and reducing the risk of human error. Containerization tools, like Docker and Kubernetes, are also crucial for PaaS integration. Containers provide a lightweight and consistent runtime environment for applications, making it easier to develop and deploy software in a PaaS platform. DevOps teams can package applications and their dependencies into containers, ensuring that they run consistently across different PaaS environments. Container orchestration tools like Kubernetes help manage containerized applications at scale, enabling efficient scaling and resource allocation in a PaaS environment. Infrastructure as code (IaC) tools, such as Terraform and Ansible, are essential for managing and provisioning resources in a PaaS environment. These tools allow DevOps teams to define infrastructure configurations as code, enabling automated provisioning of PaaS resources and infrastructure components. IaC promotes consistency, repeatability, and version control in resource management, making it easier to manage PaaS environments. Monitoring and observability tools are crucial for maintaining the health and performance of applications in a PaaS environment. Tools like Prometheus, Grafana, and Datadog provide real-time insights into application metrics, resource utilization, and system behavior. They help DevOps teams identify and address issues promptly, ensuring the reliability of applications in a PaaS platform. Security tools are paramount for ensuring the security of applications and data in a PaaS environment. DevOps teams can use security scanning tools like OWASP ZAP and SonarQube to identify vulnerabilities and code quality issues in their applications. Additionally, identity and access management (IAM) tools, such as Okta and AWS Identity and Access Management (IAM), help control access to PaaS resources and enforce security policies. Collaboration and communication tools are essential for fostering collaboration among development and operations teams in a PaaS environment. Tools like Slack, Microsoft Teams, and Atlassian Confluence facilitate real-time communication, knowledge sharing, and issue tracking. They help ensure that development and operations teams work closely together and have visibility into each other's activities. Log management and analysis tools, such as ELK Stack (Elasticsearch, Logstash, and Kibana) and Splunk, assist in collecting, aggregating, and analyzing log data from PaaS environments. These tools enable DevOps teams to troubleshoot issues, monitor application behavior, and gain valuable insights into system performance. Automation and scripting tools, like Ansible and Puppet, play a vital role in automating repetitive tasks and configurations in a PaaS environment. DevOps teams can use these tools to define infrastructure and application configurations as code, allowing for consistent and repeatable deployments. Configuration management tools, such as Chef and Puppet, help maintain the desired state of PaaS resources and ensure configuration consistency. They enable DevOps teams to automate resource provisioning, configuration changes, and updates in a PaaS environment. Testing and quality assurance tools are essential for ensuring the reliability and quality of applications in a PaaS platform. Tools like

Selenium, JUnit, and TestNG support automated testing, unit testing, and integration testing of applications in a PaaS environment. They help identify and address issues early in the development process, reducing the risk of defects in production. Version control and source code management tools, such as Git and GitHub, are fundamental for tracking changes to application code and collaborating on development projects. These tools enable DevOps teams to manage code repositories, track changes, and facilitate collaboration among developers working on PaaS applications. Workflow orchestration tools, like Apache Airflow and Apache NiFi, help automate complex workflows and data pipelines in a PaaS environment. They enable DevOps teams to design, schedule, and monitor data processing and workflow tasks in a PaaS platform. Dependency management tools, such as Maven and Gradle, assist in managing and resolving dependencies in PaaS-based projects. They ensure that the correct libraries and dependencies are included in the application, preventing compatibility issues and runtime errors. Continuous integration and continuous deployment (CI/CD) pipelines are a central component of DevOps toolchains for PaaS integration. CI/CD pipelines automate the building, testing, and deployment of applications in a PaaS environment, ensuring a rapid and reliable development cycle. These pipelines often incorporate a combination of CI/CD tools, version control systems, and testing frameworks to automate the software delivery process. In summary, DevOps tools for PaaS integration play a vital role in automating, streamlining, and optimizing the development, testing, and deployment of applications in a PaaS environment. These tools cover various aspects of the DevOps lifecycle, from continuous integration and containerization to monitoring, security, and collaboration. By leveraging the right combination of DevOps tools, organizations can effectively harness the power of PaaS platforms, accelerate software delivery, and ensure the reliability and security of their applications.

Chapter 8: Scaling and Managing PaaS Applications

Scaling your Platform as a Service (PaaS) applications is a critical aspect of ensuring that your software can handle increased workloads and deliver a consistent user experience as your business grows and evolves. The ability to scale your PaaS applications effectively allows you to meet changing demand, whether it's due to seasonal variations, unexpected traffic spikes, or the natural growth of your user base. Scaling can be accomplished in two primary ways: vertical scaling (scaling up) and horizontal scaling (scaling out). Vertical scaling involves increasing the capacity of a single server or instance by adding more resources such as CPU, memory, or storage. This approach is suitable for applications that experience moderate growth and can handle increased load by upgrading the existing infrastructure. However, vertical scaling has limitations, as there is a finite capacity to how much you can vertically scale a single server, and it may not be cost-effective in the long run. On the other hand, horizontal scaling focuses on distributing the workload across multiple instances or servers. This approach is highly scalable and allows you to handle larger workloads by adding more servers or instances to your PaaS environment. Horizontal scaling is often achieved through load balancing, where incoming requests are evenly distributed across the available instances. To effectively scale your PaaS applications horizontally, you need to consider several key factors. First, you must design your applications to be stateless, meaning that they do not rely on storing user session data or other application state on a specific server. Stateless applications can easily handle requests from multiple instances without synchronization issues. Next, you need to implement an effective load balancing strategy. Load balancers distribute incoming requests to the available instances, ensuring that no single instance becomes overloaded while others remain underutilized. Common load balancing algorithms include round-robin, least connections, and IP hash. Additionally, you should monitor the performance and resource utilization of your instances to identify bottlenecks and adjust your scaling strategy accordingly. Automated scaling is a key aspect of efficiently managing the horizontal scaling of your PaaS applications. With automated scaling, you can define rules and thresholds that trigger the addition or removal of instances based on specific performance metrics. For example, you can automatically add more instances when CPU usage exceeds a certain threshold and remove instances during periods of low traffic. Cloud providers often offer auto-scaling services that can simplify the implementation of automated scaling in your PaaS environment. Another important consideration when scaling your PaaS applications is data storage. As your application scales horizontally, you need to ensure that your data storage solution can accommodate the increased load and maintain data consistency. Distributed databases and storage solutions, such as Amazon RDS, Google Cloud SQL, or

Azure Cosmos DB, are designed to handle data storage and access in a scalable and reliable manner. You should also implement caching mechanisms to reduce the load on your database and improve application performance. Caching frequently accessed data or content at the edge of your PaaS environment can significantly reduce response times and enhance the user experience. Content delivery networks (CDNs) are commonly used for caching static assets and delivering them to users from geographically distributed locations. When it comes to scaling, it's important to consider the cost implications. Horizontal scaling can increase your infrastructure costs, as you add more instances to handle higher workloads. It's crucial to strike a balance between providing a responsive user experience and managing infrastructure expenses. To optimize costs, you can implement cost management tools and set budgets to monitor and control your spending as you scale. In addition to cost considerations, you should implement proper security measures when scaling your PaaS applications. As your application's attack surface expands with additional instances, you need to ensure that security policies, access controls, and threat detection mechanisms are in place. Implementing a web application firewall (WAF) and regularly conducting security audits can help protect your application from potential threats. Furthermore, you should consider disaster recovery and high availability strategies when scaling your PaaS applications. Distributed architectures should incorporate redundancy and failover mechanisms to ensure that your application remains available even in the event of instance failures or other disruptions. Implementing automated backup and recovery processes is essential for maintaining data integrity and minimizing downtime. Finally, it's essential to regularly test and validate your scaling strategies through load testing and performance monitoring. Testing helps you identify performance bottlenecks and fine-tune your scaling configurations to ensure that your PaaS applications can handle peak loads. Regularly reviewing and optimizing your scaling approach is a continuous process that ensures your applications remain responsive and reliable as your business grows. In summary, scaling your PaaS applications is a critical aspect of effectively managing the growth and demand of your software. Horizontal scaling, combined with stateless application design, load balancing, automated scaling, and a robust data storage strategy, allows you to handle increased workloads efficiently. Consider cost management, security, disaster recovery, and performance testing as integral components of your scaling strategy to ensure that your PaaS applications deliver a consistent and reliable user experience as your business evolves.

Effective management of Platform as a Service (PaaS) environments is crucial for organizations seeking to harness the benefits of cloud computing while maintaining operational efficiency. PaaS environments provide a flexible and scalable foundation for developing, deploying, and managing applications, but they require careful planning and ongoing oversight. One key aspect of PaaS management is resource *allocation and utilization. Organizations must monitor and allocate resources such as compute power, memory, and storage effectively to ensure optimal application performance. Resource allocation should align with the requirements of each application, taking into account factors like traffic, processing demands, and storage needs. Efficiently managing resources helps avoid overprovisioning, which can lead to unnecessary costs, or underprovisioning, which can result in performance issues. Another critical aspect of PaaS management is security. Organizations must implement robust security measures to protect their applications, data, and infrastructure in the PaaS environment. This includes configuring access controls, encryption, and identity and access management (IAM) to ensure that only authorized users have access to resources. Security audits, vulnerability assessments, and intrusion detection systems help organizations identify and mitigate potential security threats. Monitoring and observability play a significant role in effective PaaS management. Continuous monitoring of applications and infrastructure provides real-time insights into performance, resource utilization, and potential issues. Monitoring tools track metrics, logs, and traces, allowing organizations to detect anomalies, troubleshoot problems, and optimize application performance. Observability extends monitoring by providing deeper insights into application behavior, facilitating root cause analysis, and enhancing overall system reliability. Automation is a key element of effective PaaS management. Automation tools and scripts help streamline repetitive tasks such as provisioning, scaling, and deployment. By automating these processes, organizations can reduce manual intervention, minimize errors, and improve operational efficiency. DevOps practices, which emphasize automation and collaboration between development and operations teams, are often integrated into PaaS management strategies. Effective cost management is essential when managing PaaS environments. Organizations should closely monitor their cloud spending and optimize resource utilization to control costs. This includes setting budgets, implementing cost tracking, and utilizing cloud cost management tools provided by cloud providers. Resource tagging and cost allocation can help organizations allocate costs to specific projects or departments, improving transparency and accountability. Another important consideration in PaaS management is compliance. Organizations must ensure that their PaaS environments comply with industry regulations and internal policies related to data privacy, security, and governance. Regular compliance audits and assessments are essential to demonstrate adherence to these standards. Additionally, organizations should have well-defined disaster recovery and business continuity plans in place to mitigate the impact of unexpected events. These plans include backup and recovery procedures, data replication, and failover mechanisms to ensure that applications remain available in the event of system failures or disasters. Capacity planning is an integral part of PaaS management. Organizations should anticipate future growth and assess their capacity needs to ensure that their PaaS environments can scale to accommodate increased workloads. Scaling strategies should align with application requirements and traffic patterns, allowing organizations to add or remove resources as needed. Effective management of PaaS environments also involves governance and policy enforcement. Establishing clear governance policies and practices helps organizations maintain control over their cloud resources. This includes defining roles and responsibilities, enforcing access controls, and implementing policies for resource provisioning and deprovisioning. Effective governance ensures that cloud resources are used efficiently and securely. Collaboration and communication are critical components of PaaS management. Effective cross-functional collaboration between development, operations, security, and other teams helps organizations make informed decisions and address challenges promptly. Collaboration tools, chat platforms, and shared documentation facilitate communication and knowledge sharing among team members. Change management is another consideration in PaaS management. Organizations should have processes in place to manage and track changes to their PaaS environments, including version control and configuration management. Change management ensures that modifications to applications and infrastructure are well-documented and do not introduce disruptions or vulnerabilities. Training and skill development are essential for building a capable and knowledgeable team for PaaS management. Investing in training programs and upskilling initiatives ensures that staff members have the expertise needed to effectively manage and operate within the PaaS environment. Staying informed about updates and enhancements offered by the PaaS provider is crucial for effective management. Organizations should regularly assess whether new features and capabilities can benefit their applications and operations. Adopting a culture of continuous improvement encourages organizations to adapt their management strategies in response to evolving business goals and technological advancements. In summary, effective management of PaaS environments requires a holistic approach that encompasses resource allocation, security, monitoring, automation, cost management, compliance, disaster recovery, capacity planning, governance, collaboration, change management, training, and a commitment to continuous improvement. By addressing these aspects, organizations can maximize the benefits of their PaaS environments while maintaining operational excellence and achieving their business objectives in the cloud.*

Chapter 9: Security and Compliance in PaaS

Ensuring security in a Platform as a Service (PaaS) environment is a fundamental concern for organizations that rely on cloud-based platforms to develop, deploy, and manage their applications. PaaS providers offer robust security features, but it is essential for organizations to take proactive steps to protect their data, applications, and infrastructure. One of the key principles of PaaS security is the shared responsibility model. Under this model, the cloud provider is responsible for securing the underlying infrastructure, while the organization using the PaaS platform is responsible for securing their applications and data. This shared responsibility requires organizations to implement security measures specific to their PaaS deployments. Access control is a critical aspect of PaaS security. Organizations should define and enforce strict access controls to ensure that only authorized personnel can access PaaS resources. This includes implementing role-based access control (RBAC) and multi-factor authentication (MFA) to enhance security. Additionally, organizations should regularly review and update access permissions to align with changing roles and responsibilities. Data encryption is essential for protecting data at rest and in transit in a PaaS environment. Organizations should use encryption techniques such as HTTPS/TLS for data in transit and encryption at rest for data stored in databases or file storage. Data encryption ensures that even if an unauthorized party gains access to the data, they cannot read it without the decryption keys. Security monitoring and auditing are crucial for detecting and responding to security incidents in real-time. Organizations should implement robust monitoring and auditing tools that track user activities, access patterns, and system events. These tools help identify suspicious behavior and potential security breaches. Regularly reviewing and analyzing security logs is essential for prompt incident response. Vulnerability management is an ongoing process to identify, assess, and remediate vulnerabilities in PaaS applications and infrastructure. Organizations should conduct regular vulnerability scans and assessments to identify security weaknesses. Once vulnerabilities are identified, organizations should prioritize and remediate them promptly to reduce the risk of exploitation. Patch management is a critical component of PaaS security. Organizations should apply security patches and updates to both the operating system and the software components used in their PaaS environments. Outdated software can be a target for attackers, so staying up to date is essential. Secure development practices are essential for building and deploying secure applications in a PaaS environment. Organizations should implement secure coding standards, conduct code reviews, and use static and dynamic application security testing (SAST and DAST) tools. Security should be integrated into the software development lifecycle (SDLC) from the initial design phase to deployment. Identity and access management

(IAM) is vital for controlling user access to PaaS resources. Organizations should implement IAM solutions to manage user identities, access policies, and privileges. IAM helps enforce the principle of least privilege, ensuring that users have access only to the resources necessary for their roles. Security awareness and training programs are essential for educating employees and stakeholders about security best practices and threats. Organizations should provide security training to all personnel who have access to PaaS environments. Security awareness helps reduce the risk of social engineering attacks and human errors that can lead to security breaches. Incident response and disaster recovery plans are critical for mitigating the impact of security incidents in a PaaS environment. Organizations should develop and test incident response plans to ensure they can respond effectively to security breaches or other incidents. Additionally, disaster recovery plans should be in place to minimize downtime and data loss in the event of a catastrophic event. Regular security assessments and penetration testing help organizations identify and address security weaknesses in their PaaS environments. Security assessments involve comprehensive evaluations of security controls, policies, and procedures. Penetration testing simulates real-world attacks to identify vulnerabilities that could be exploited by malicious actors. Compliance with industry regulations and standards is essential for organizations that handle sensitive data in their PaaS environments. Organizations should understand and comply with relevant

regulations, such as GDPR, HIPAA, or PCI DSS. Compliance frameworks provide guidelines for securing data and maintaining privacy. Cloud security best practices should be followed when deploying applications and data in a PaaS environment. Organizations should consider the shared responsibility model and apply security measures to their applications and data accordingly. This includes securing configurations, implementing firewalls, and using intrusion detection and prevention systems (IDPS) as needed. Regular security assessments of third-party components and integrations are essential for identifying and addressing vulnerabilities introduced by third-party software or services. Organizations should conduct due diligence when selecting third-party components and continuously monitor their security posture. Security automation and orchestration can help organizations improve their security posture in a PaaS environment. Automated security tools can identify and respond to security threats more rapidly and efficiently than manual processes. Security orchestration enables organizations to automate incident response workflows. In summary, ensuring PaaS security is a shared responsibility between the organization and the PaaS provider. Organizations must implement security measures such as access control, encryption, monitoring, vulnerability management, patch management, secure development practices, IAM, security awareness, incident response, and compliance. By following these principles and best practices, organizations can enhance the security of their PaaS environments and protect their applications and data from potential threats and vulnerabilities. Compliance considerations in a Platform as a Service (PaaS) environment are of paramount importance for organizations that handle sensitive data or operate in regulated industries. Compliance refers to the adherence to specific rules, regulations, standards, and industry guidelines that govern data protection, security, privacy, and other aspects of business operations. In PaaS, organizations need to navigate a complex landscape of compliance requirements to ensure that their PaaS deployments meet legal and industry-specific obligations. One of the fundamental aspects of compliance in PaaS is understanding the shared responsibility model. Under this model, cloud providers are responsible for the security and compliance of the underlying infrastructure, while organizations are responsible for securing their applications and data. Organizations must be aware of what aspects of compliance are covered by their PaaS provider and what responsibilities they retain. The General Data Protection Regulation (GDPR) is a significant compliance consideration for organizations that handle personal data, especially if they operate in the European Union (EU) or process data from EU citizens. GDPR sets stringent requirements for data protection, including consent management, data breach notification, and the right to be forgotten. Organizations need to ensure that their PaaS environments comply with GDPR's data protection principles and requirements. The Health Insurance Portability and

Accountability Act (HIPAA) is another critical compliance framework for organizations in the healthcare industry. HIPAA mandates strict safeguards for the protection of patients' healthcare information, known as protected health information (PHI). Organizations must implement security measures, such as encryption, access controls, and audit trails, to protect PHI in their PaaS environments. Payment Card Industry Data Security Standard (PCI DSS) compliance is essential for organizations that handle credit card data. PCI DSS outlines requirements for securing payment card data, including encryption, access controls, vulnerability management, and regular security assessments. Organizations must ensure that their PaaS environments comply with PCI DSS to protect cardholder data. The Sarbanes-Oxley Act (SOX) is a compliance framework that focuses on financial reporting and corporate governance. Publicly traded companies must adhere to SOX regulations to maintain accurate financial records and prevent fraud. Organizations should consider how their PaaS deployments affect financial data and implement controls to comply with SOX requirements. The Federal Risk and Authorization Management Program (FedRAMP) is a U.S. government program that standardizes security assessments and authorizations for cloud service providers. Organizations seeking to provide PaaS solutions to federal agencies need to obtain FedRAMP authorization, ensuring that their services meet government security standards. In addition to these specific compliance frameworks, organizations should also be aware of industry-specific regulations. For example, the financial services industry is subject to regulations like the Dodd-Frank Wall Street Reform and Consumer Protection Act. Energy companies need to adhere to regulations such as the North American Electric Reliability Corporation (NERC) standards. Retail organizations must consider Payment Application Data Security Standard (PA-DSS) compliance for point-of-sale systems. Compliance considerations in PaaS also extend to data sovereignty and localization. Different countries and regions have specific data protection laws that govern where data can be stored and processed. Organizations must ensure that their PaaS provider complies with these regulations to avoid potential legal issues. Data encryption is a fundamental component of compliance in PaaS. Organizations should encrypt sensitive data at rest and in transit to protect it from unauthorized access. Encryption helps organizations meet data protection requirements and safeguard sensitive information. Access controls are essential for ensuring that only authorized personnel can access PaaS resources and data. Role-based access control (RBAC) and multi-factor authentication (MFA) should be implemented to enforce access policies. Regular audits and assessments are necessary to verify compliance with regulatory requirements. Organizations should conduct internal and external audits, security assessments, and vulnerability scans to identify and address compliance gaps. Documentation and record-keeping are vital for demonstrating compliance. Organizations should maintain thorough records of their compliance efforts, including policies, procedures, assessments, and audit reports. These records help prove adherence to regulations during compliance audits. Incorporating compliance into the software development lifecycle (SDLC) is essential for PaaS environments. Secure coding practices, code reviews, and vulnerability assessments should be integrated into the development process to identify and mitigate security and compliance risks early. Compliance is an ongoing effort that requires continuous monitoring and adaptation. Regulations and industry standards evolve, and organizations must stay up to date with changes that may affect their PaaS deployments. Engaging legal counsel or compliance experts can provide valuable guidance in navigating the complex landscape of compliance in PaaS. In summary, compliance considerations are a critical aspect of managing PaaS environments, especially for organizations that handle sensitive data or operate in regulated industries. Understanding the shared responsibility model, complying with specific regulations and industry standards, implementing security controls, conducting audits, and maintaining documentation are all essential components of a robust compliance program in PaaS. By addressing these considerations, organizations can build trust with customers, avoid legal and financial penalties, and ensure the security and privacy of their data and applications in the cloud.

Chapter 10: Future Trends in PaaS and Cloud Computing

Emerging trends in Platform as a Service (PaaS) are reshaping the landscape of cloud computing and application development. As technology continues to evolve, PaaS offerings and practices are evolving with it, providing new opportunities and challenges for organizations. One significant trend in PaaS is the increasing adoption of serverless computing. Serverless platforms, such as AWS Lambda, Azure Functions, and Google Cloud Functions, allow developers to build and deploy applications without managing underlying server infrastructure. This trend simplifies application development, as developers can focus solely on writing code and defining functions, leaving the operational aspects to the cloud provider. Serverless computing offers benefits such as automatic scaling, reduced infrastructure management, and cost savings based on actual usage. Another emerging trend is the growing importance of containerization and container orchestration in PaaS environments. Containers, powered by technologies like Docker, provide a consistent and portable way to package and run applications and their dependencies. Container orchestration platforms like Kubernetes enable organizations to manage and scale containerized applications efficiently. This trend is driven by the need for agility and flexibility in deploying and managing applications across diverse environments, from on-

premises data centers to multiple cloud providers. Edge computing is also gaining prominence in the PaaS landscape. Edge computing extends cloud capabilities to the edge of the network, closer to where data is generated and consumed. This trend addresses the need for low-latency and real-time processing, making it suitable for applications like IoT, autonomous vehicles, and content delivery. PaaS providers are expanding their offerings to include edge computing capabilities, allowing organizations to develop and deploy edge applications more easily. Artificial intelligence (AI) and machine learning (ML) integration is becoming increasingly prevalent in PaaS platforms. PaaS providers are offering AI/ML services that enable developers to incorporate machine learning models and capabilities into their applications. These services include natural language processing, computer vision, and predictive analytics, making it easier for organizations to leverage AI and ML in their applications. Hybrid and multi-cloud strategies are on the rise in PaaS adoption. Organizations are seeking flexibility by combining on-premises infrastructure with multiple cloud providers to meet their specific needs. PaaS providers are responding by offering tools and services that facilitate hybrid and multi-cloud deployments, enabling seamless application portability and management across environments. Security and compliance in PaaS are evolving as critical concerns. With the increasing complexity of cloud environments, organizations are placing a stronger emphasis on security best practices, identity and access management, and compliance with industry regulations.

PaaS providers are enhancing their security offerings, providing tools and services to help organizations safeguard their applications and data. Microservices architecture is shaping the way applications are developed and deployed in PaaS environments. Microservices break down complex applications into smaller, independent services that can be developed, deployed, and scaled separately. This architectural trend aligns with the agility and scalability requirements of modern applications and allows organizations to innovate faster. Blockchain technology is starting to find its place in PaaS. PaaS providers are offering blockchain-as-a-service (BaaS) solutions that simplify the development and deployment of blockchain applications. These solutions enable organizations to experiment with blockchain technology without the complexities of managing a blockchain network. Quantum computing is an emerging frontier in PaaS. Although still in its infancy, quantum computing has the potential to revolutionize computing power and solve complex problems that are currently beyond the reach of classical computers. PaaS providers are exploring quantum computing capabilities and offering quantum services to developers. Serverless containers are gaining traction as a fusion of serverless and containerization trends. Serverless container platforms, like AWS Fargate and Azure Container Instances, enable organizations to run containers without managing the underlying infrastructure, combining the benefits of both approaches. Low-code and no-code development platforms are democratizing application development.

These platforms allow business users and non-developers to create applications with minimal coding, accelerating the development process and reducing the IT skills barrier. DevSecOps, a fusion of development, security, and operations practices, is becoming integral to PaaS environments. It emphasizes security as a fundamental aspect of the development and operations lifecycle, enabling organizations to build secure and resilient applications. Environmental sustainability is emerging as a social responsibility in PaaS. As organizations become more conscious of their environmental impact, they are seeking PaaS providers that prioritize sustainability through energy-efficient data centers and renewable energy sources. In summary, emerging trends in PaaS reflect the evolving needs and opportunities in cloud computing and application development. Serverless computing, containerization, edge computing, AI/ML integration, hybrid and multi-cloud strategies, security, microservices, blockchain, quantum computing, serverless containers, low-code/no-code development, DevSecOps, and environmental sustainability are shaping the future of PaaS. Organizations that stay informed and adapt to these trends will be better positioned to leverage the full potential of PaaS in their digital transformation journeys. The landscape of cloud computing has undergone significant evolution over the years, reshaping how businesses and individuals interact with technology and data. Cloud computing, as a concept, has its roots in the 1960s, but it wasn't until the early 2000s that it began to gain widespread attention and adoption. The evolution of cloud computing can be traced through several distinct phases, each marked by technological advancements, changing paradigms, and shifting business models. The first phase of cloud computing was characterized by the emergence of Infrastructure as a Service (IaaS) providers. During this period, companies like Amazon Web Services (AWS) and Microsoft Azure pioneered the idea of providing virtualized infrastructure resources over the internet. This innovation allowed organizations to rent computing power, storage, and networking on-demand, without the need to invest in physical hardware. IaaS providers laid the foundation for scalable and cost-effective cloud computing. The second phase of cloud computing saw the rise of Platform as a Service (PaaS) offerings. PaaS providers, such as Google App Engine and Heroku, introduced a higher-level abstraction for developers. They provided tools and frameworks that allowed developers to focus on building and deploying applications without worrying about the underlying infrastructure. This phase emphasized developer productivity and streamlined application deployment. The third phase marked the advent of Software as a Service (SaaS) applications. Companies like Salesforce, Google Workspace (formerly G Suite), and Dropbox delivered software applications directly over the internet. SaaS eliminated the need for users to install and maintain software on their local devices, making it accessible from any internet-connected device. This phase brought about the concept of subscription-based software licensing, disrupting traditional software distribution models. The fourth phase of cloud computing introduced the idea of Function as a Service (FaaS), often referred to as serverless computing. Serverless platforms, such as AWS Lambda and Azure Functions, abstracted away the concept of servers entirely. Developers could now focus on writing code in the form of functions, which were executed in response to events. Serverless computing introduced greater flexibility and efficiency in application development. As cloud computing continued to evolve, hybrid and multi-cloud strategies emerged as a response to the growing complexity of cloud environments. Organizations began combining on-premises infrastructure with multiple cloud providers to meet specific business needs. This approach provided greater flexibility, redundancy, and disaster recovery capabilities. The sixth phase of cloud computing centered on edge computing. Edge computing extended cloud capabilities to the edge of the network, closer to where data was generated. This trend aimed to reduce latency and enable real-time processing for applications like the Internet of Things (IoT) and autonomous vehicles. Edge computing brought cloud-like capabilities to distributed, remote locations. Artificial intelligence (AI) and machine learning (ML) integration became prominent in cloud computing. Cloud providers started offering AI/ML services, enabling organizations to leverage machine learning models and capabilities within their applications. These services included natural language processing, computer vision, and predictive analytics, making AI/ML more accessible. Security and *compliance took center stage in the evolving landscape of cloud computing. With the increased complexity of cloud environments, organizations prioritized security best practices, identity and access management, and compliance with industry regulations. Cloud providers responded by enhancing their security offerings and providing tools and services to help organizations safeguard their applications and data. Automation and orchestration became fundamental for managing cloud resources efficiently. Automation tools and practices allowed organizations to streamline provisioning, scaling, and deployment processes. Cloud providers introduced orchestration platforms like Kubernetes to manage containerized applications at scale. Quantum computing started to make its presence felt in cloud computing. Though still in its infancy, quantum computing held the promise of revolutionizing computing power and solving complex problems. Cloud providers explored quantum computing capabilities, offering quantum services for developers. Serverless containers emerged as a fusion of serverless and containerization trends. Serverless container platforms allowed organizations to run containers without managing underlying infrastructure, combining the benefits of both approaches. Low-code and no-code development platforms democratized application development. These platforms empowered business users and non-developers to create applications with minimal coding, accelerating the development process and reducing IT skills barriers. DevSecOps, an amalgamation of development, security, and operations practices, became integral to cloud computing. It emphasized security as a fundamental aspect of the development and operations lifecycle, enabling organizations to build secure and resilient applications. Environmental sustainability gained importance as a social responsibility in cloud computing. Organizations sought cloud providers that prioritized sustainability through energy-efficient data centers and renewable energy sources. In summary, the evolving landscape of cloud computing reflects a journey of technological innovation, changing paradigms, and shifting business models. From the early phases of IaaS and PaaS to the emergence of serverless computing, hybrid and multi-cloud strategies, edge computing, AI/ML integration, security, compliance, automation, quantum computing, serverless containers, low-code/no-code development, DevSecOps, and environmental sustainability, cloud computing continues to transform the way we interact with technology and data. Organizations that adapt to these evolving trends will be better positioned to leverage the full potential of cloud computing in their digital transformation journeys.*

BOOK 2
Cloud Powerhouse
Mastering PaaS with Google, Azure, and IBM

ROB BOTWRIGHT

Chapter 1: The Evolution of Cloud Computing and PaaS

Cloud computing, a transformative technology, has reshaped the digital landscape over the past few decades. It has emerged as a powerful force, altering the way individuals, businesses, and governments store, access, and manage data and applications. The roots of cloud computing can be traced back to the 1950s when early mainframe computers laid the foundation for the concept. However, it wasn't until the late 1990s and early 2000s that cloud computing began to take its modern shape. One of the pioneering moments in this journey was the launch of Salesforce.com in 1999, which introduced the concept of delivering software as a service (SaaS) over the internet. This breakthrough marked the beginning of a shift away from traditional software deployment models. In 2002, Amazon Web Services (AWS) entered the scene, revolutionizing the infrastructure landscape by offering cloud-based computing and storage services. AWS set the stage for the rapid growth of cloud computing, enabling businesses to scale their operations with unprecedented flexibility. Around the same time, Google unveiled its search engine, Gmail, and Google Maps, showcasing the power of cloud-based applications. Microsoft, a tech giant, recognized the potential of cloud computing and introduced Azure in 2010, providing a comprehensive cloud platform for businesses. These developments marked a pivotal moment as major tech players began embracing cloud computing as a core component of their strategies. As cloud computing gained momentum, it started to reshape the IT industry, leading to increased competition and innovation. The year 2013 witnessed the rise of Docker, a containerization technology that streamlined application deployment and management, making it more efficient. Docker containers played a vital role in enabling developers to build and deploy applications across diverse environments with ease. Meanwhile, the concept of serverless computing gained traction, with AWS Lambda introducing a new paradigm in cloud computing. Serverless computing allowed developers to focus solely on writing code, abstracting away infrastructure management. As cloud providers continued to enhance their services, data privacy and security became significant concerns. The proliferation of data breaches and cyberattacks highlighted the need for robust security measures in cloud environments. The adoption of multi-cloud and hybrid cloud strategies emerged as viable solutions to address these security concerns. In 2018, the European Union implemented the General Data Protection Regulation (GDPR), imposing stringent data protection requirements on businesses handling personal data. GDPR forced organizations to reevaluate their data handling practices, particularly in the context of cloud storage and processing. The year 2020 brought unforeseen challenges in the form of the COVID-19 pandemic, which accelerated the shift to remote work and reliance on cloud-based collaboration tools. Cloud computing proved to be a lifeline for businesses, enabling remote access to critical resources and facilitating communication and collaboration. The pandemic underscored the importance of cloud resilience and the need for disaster recovery and business continuity planning. The rapid adoption of cloud-based video conferencing and communication tools, such as Zoom and Microsoft Teams, demonstrated the scalability and adaptability of cloud services. In 2021, the emergence of edge computing gained prominence as organizations sought to reduce latency and enhance real-time processing capabilities. Edge computing leverages cloud resources closer to the data source, enabling faster response times for applications and services. Artificial intelligence and machine learning continued to be integrated with cloud computing, empowering organizations to derive valuable insights from their data. Cloud providers introduced specialized AI and ML services, making it easier for businesses to develop and deploy intelligent applications. Sustainability became a significant focus in the cloud computing industry, with a growing emphasis on reducing carbon footprints and achieving energy efficiency. Renewable energy initiatives and data center optimizations were undertaken to minimize the environmental impact of cloud infrastructure. As we look ahead, the future of cloud computing appears promising, with ongoing innovations and advancements on the horizon. Quantum computing, for instance, holds the potential to revolutionize cloud-based processing, solving complex problems at unprecedented speeds. The evolution of 5G networks is set to further enhance the capabilities of cloud computing, enabling low-latency, high-bandwidth connections. The convergence of cloud computing with other emerging technologies, such as blockchain and augmented reality, promises new opportunities and applications. The journey of cloud computing has been a remarkable one, from its humble beginnings to becoming the cornerstone of modern digital transformation. It has enabled businesses to scale, innovate, and adapt in an ever-changing technological landscape. Cloud computing has empowered individuals, organizations, and governments to harness the power of data and technology to drive progress and innovation. It has transcended industries and borders, shaping the way we live, work, and connect in the digital age. In closing, the historical milestones in cloud computing have paved the way for an exciting and dynamic future, where the possibilities are limited only by our imagination and creativity. Platform as a Service, or PaaS, emerged as a vital component in the evolution of cloud computing. PaaS represents a model that offers a cloud platform and environment for developers to build, deploy, and manage applications. The concept of PaaS can be traced back to the mid-2000s when cloud computing was still in its infancy. At that time, infrastructure as a service (IaaS) and software as a service (SaaS) were the primary cloud service models available. The need for a more developer-centric cloud solution became apparent as companies sought ways to streamline application development and delivery. One of the early pioneers in the PaaS space was Google App Engine, which was launched in 2008. Google's platform allowed developers to build and host web applications using familiar programming languages like Python and Java. This marked a significant departure from traditional development methods, which often required extensive infrastructure setup and maintenance. Around the same time, Microsoft introduced Windows Azure, later known as Microsoft Azure, in 2010. Azure provided a comprehensive PaaS offering along with support for various programming languages, tools, and frameworks. These early entrants into the PaaS market set the stage for a broader shift in the industry. Developers began to appreciate the advantages of PaaS, such as simplified application scaling, automatic infrastructure management, and reduced time to market. PaaS platforms also offered features like database services, identity management, and development tools that simplified the development process. As PaaS gained traction, other major cloud providers, including Amazon Web Services (AWS) and IBM, entered the market with their own PaaS offerings. Each provider tailored their platform to suit different developer needs and application requirements. For example, AWS Elastic Beanstalk simplified the deployment of web applications, while IBM Cloud Foundry offered an open-source PaaS solution. As PaaS continued to grow, it found adoption in various industries and use cases. Enterprises embraced PaaS for its ability to accelerate digital transformation and innovation. Developers no longer had to worry about infrastructure provisioning and management, allowing them to focus on writing code and building features. The flexibility of PaaS platforms meant that applications could be developed using a wide range of programming languages and frameworks. PaaS also enabled DevOps practices, promoting collaboration between development and operations teams for faster and more reliable application delivery. In the healthcare industry, PaaS played a critical role in accelerating the development of healthcare applications and services. Healthcare providers leveraged PaaS to build and deploy applications that improved patient care, streamlined administrative processes, and enhanced data security. Similarly, in the financial sector, PaaS platforms facilitated the development of fintech applications, online banking systems, and trading platforms. These platforms offered the scalability and reliability required to handle high-volume transactions and data processing. In the world of e-commerce, PaaS became instrumental in building and scaling online marketplaces, enabling businesses to handle seasonal spikes in traffic and demand. The gaming industry also benefited from PaaS, with game developers using cloud platforms to build and host multiplayer games, leaderboards, and in-game analytics. PaaS solutions were not limited to startups and tech giants; they were embraced by educational institutions, government agencies, and non-profit organizations. These entities used PaaS to create e-learning platforms, government services, and charitable applications. The growth of PaaS was further fueled by the emergence of microservices architecture and containerization technologies like Docker. These developments allowed developers to break down applications into smaller, manageable components and deploy them independently. PaaS providers adapted to this trend by offering container orchestration services like Kubernetes, making it easier to deploy and manage containerized applications. The integration of PaaS with container orchestration opened up new possibilities for building and scaling cloud-native applications. Serverless computing, a serverless PaaS model, also gained prominence, enabling developers to run code in response to events without worrying about server management. Serverless platforms, like AWS Lambda and Azure Functions, offered a pay-as-you-go pricing model, reducing infrastructure costs. As PaaS continued to evolve, it incorporated artificial intelligence and machine learning capabilities, enabling developers to infuse their applications with intelligent features. These AI-powered services ranged from speech recognition and natural language processing to computer vision and recommendation systems. In 2020, the COVID-19 pandemic accelerated digital transformation across industries, and PaaS played a pivotal role in enabling remote work and online services. Organizations turned to cloud platforms to build and deploy applications that supported remote collaboration, telehealth, and e-commerce. PaaS providers responded by enhancing their offerings to meet the increased demand for scalable and reliable solutions. As we look to the future, PaaS is poised to remain a critical enabler of innovation and agility. The continued development of cloud-native technologies, such as serverless computing and Kubernetes, will further shape the PaaS landscape. PaaS *will continue to empower developers to create applications that leverage the full potential of the cloud. It will play a key role in industries like healthcare, finance, e-commerce, and entertainment, driving the development of new and transformative applications. In summary, the birth and growth of Platform as a Service (PaaS) have been instrumental in revolutionizing application development and deployment. PaaS has empowered developers and organizations to embrace the cloud, accelerate digital transformation, and drive innovation across diverse sectors. As technology continues to evolve, PaaS will adapt and thrive, supporting the ever-expanding landscape of cloud-native applications and services.*

Chapter 2: A Deep Dive into Google Cloud Platform (GCP)

Google Cloud Platform (GCP) offers a comprehensive suite of core infrastructure services that form the foundation for a wide range of cloud-based applications and solutions. These core services provide the essential building blocks necessary to create, deploy, and manage cloud resources effectively. At the heart of GCP's core infrastructure services is Google's global network, which underpins the reliability and scalability of all GCP services. This extensive, high-performance network connects data centers around the world, ensuring low-latency, secure, and redundant connectivity for GCP customers. GCP's Compute Engine service allows users to run virtual machines (VMs) on Google's infrastructure, providing flexibility and control over compute resources. Customers can choose from a variety of VM types to meet their specific performance and configuration requirements. Google Kubernetes Engine (GKE) is a managed container orchestration service that simplifies the deployment and management of containerized applications using Kubernetes. GKE automates many aspects of cluster management, making it easier for developers to focus on application development. Cloud Functions is GCP's serverless computing service, enabling developers to run code in response to events without managing server infrastructure. With Cloud Functions, developers can build lightweight, event-driven applications that scale automatically based on demand. GCP offers several storage services, including Cloud Storage for object storage, Cloud SQL for managed relational databases, and Cloud Bigtable for NoSQL databases. These services provide scalable and reliable storage solutions to meet various data storage needs. BigQuery, GCP's fully managed, serverless data warehouse, enables users to analyze and query large datasets with high performance and scalability. It supports SQL-like queries and integrates with other GCP services for data analysis and machine learning. Networking plays a crucial role in GCP's core infrastructure, with services like Virtual Private Cloud (VPC) for creating isolated, private networks and Cloud Load Balancing for distributing traffic across instances and services. VPC peering allows secure communication between different VPCs, and Cloud Interconnect provides dedicated network connections to GCP. Identity and Access Management (IAM) is a critical component of GCP's security model, allowing users to control access to resources and data. IAM enables fine-grained access control and provides auditing and monitoring capabilities to enhance security. GCP's Stackdriver Monitoring and Logging services offer comprehensive observability into the performance and health of applications and infrastructure. These services provide real-time monitoring, alerting, and logging to help operators and developers troubleshoot and optimize their environments. Google Cloud also offers a range of security services, including the Google Cloud Security

Command Center (Cloud SCC), which provides security risk and compliance management across GCP resources. Cloud Identity-Aware Proxy (IAP) adds an additional layer of security by controlling access to applications based on identity and context. GCP's core infrastructure services support hybrid and multi-cloud deployments through partnerships with leading networking and security providers. Customers can extend their on-premises environments to GCP using dedicated interconnects and VPNs. In addition to core infrastructure services, GCP offers a wide array of data storage and processing services that enable organizations to harness the power of their data. Cloud Datastore is a fully managed NoSQL database service designed for high availability and scalability. Cloud Spanner is a globally distributed, horizontally scalable database service that combines the benefits of traditional relational databases with the flexibility of NoSQL. Bigtable, as mentioned earlier, is a scalable NoSQL database service that excels at handling large volumes of data with low-latency read and write access. Cloud Storage, in addition to being a core infrastructure service, serves as a highly available and durable object storage solution for a variety of use cases. Google Cloud Pub/Sub provides reliable, real-time messaging between applications, enabling event-driven architectures and data streaming. Cloud Dataprep is a fully managed data preparation service that helps clean, transform, and visualize data for analytics and machine learning. Cloud Composer is a managed workflow orchestration service built on Apache Airflow, allowing users to automate and schedule data workflows. Dataflow is a fully managed stream and batch data processing service that enables real-time analytics and ETL (Extract, Transform, Load) tasks. BigQuery, with its powerful SQL-like query capabilities, is not only a data warehousing solution but also a data analytics and exploration tool. Google Cloud's machine learning services are part of its broader suite of data and analytics offerings. Cloud AI Platform allows data scientists and machine learning engineers to build, train, and deploy machine learning models at scale. AutoML provides a user-friendly interface for building custom machine learning models without extensive coding or machine learning expertise. Cloud TPU (Tensor Processing Unit) is a specialized hardware accelerator for machine learning workloads that delivers high-performance inference and training capabilities. AI Hub serves as a collaborative repository for machine learning assets, including datasets, notebooks, and models. GCP's core infrastructure services, coupled with its data and analytics capabilities, provide organizations with a robust and flexible platform for innovation. Customers across various industries, from healthcare to finance to retail, leverage GCP's services to drive digital transformation and gain a competitive edge. Whether it's building cloud-native applications, running data analytics, or developing machine learning solutions, GCP's core infrastructure services form the foundation for creating modern, scalable, and reliable cloud-based solutions. Google offers a diverse range of Platform as a Service (PaaS) offerings that cater to the needs of developers, businesses, and enterprises. These PaaS *services provide a streamlined and efficient way to develop, deploy, and manage applications in the cloud. One of Google's flagship PaaS offerings is Google App Engine, which allows developers to build and deploy applications without worrying about infrastructure management. App Engine supports multiple programming languages, making it accessible to a wide range of developers. Google Kubernetes Engine (GKE) is another powerful PaaS offering that simplifies container orchestration using Kubernetes. With GKE, organizations can effortlessly manage containerized applications and scale them based on demand. Cloud Functions, Google's serverless computing platform, offers a flexible environment for running event-driven code. Developers can trigger functions in response to events and pay only for the compute resources used during execution. Google Cloud Run extends the serverless concept to containerized applications, allowing developers to deploy and manage container workloads without the complexity of managing the underlying infrastructure. Cloud Run autoscales the containers based on incoming requests, making it easy to handle varying workloads. For organizations looking to build data-intensive applications, Google Cloud Dataflow is a fully managed stream and batch data processing service. It enables real-time analytics and ETL (Extract, Transform, Load) tasks, making it a valuable tool for data engineering and analytics pipelines. Google Cloud Functions for Firebase is a specialized PaaS offering for mobile and web developers. It allows developers to create serverless functions that can be triggered by Firebase services, such as authentication and Firestore database events. Firebase also includes features like real-time database synchronization and hosting for web applications. Google Cloud Composer is a managed workflow orchestration service based on the popular Apache Airflow framework. It helps organizations automate and schedule data workflows, making it easier to manage complex data pipelines and ETL processes. In the world of machine learning and AI, Google's Cloud AI Platform offers a comprehensive suite of tools and services. Data scientists and machine learning engineers can use this platform to build, train, and deploy machine learning models at scale. AutoML, part of Cloud AI Platform, is designed for users who want to create custom machine learning models without extensive coding or machine learning expertise. Cloud AI Platform also provides support for distributed training and hyperparameter tuning to improve model performance. Cloud Machine Learning Engine, another component of Cloud AI Platform, offers a serverless managed environment for running TensorFlow-based machine learning workloads. Google Cloud TPU (Tensor Processing Unit) accelerates machine learning workloads by providing custom hardware designed specifically for AI tasks. Developers can harness the power of TPUs to train and deploy machine learning models with high performance and efficiency. To facilitate collaborative machine learning projects, Google offers AI Hub, a repository for machine learning assets, including datasets, notebooks, and models. AI Hub streamlines the sharing and discovery of machine learning resources within organizations.*

Google Cloud's PaaS offerings extend beyond application development and machine learning to encompass data and analytics services. BigQuery, a fully managed, serverless data warehouse, enables organizations to analyze and query large datasets with high performance and scalability. It supports standard SQL-like queries and integrates seamlessly with other GCP services for data analysis and machine learning. Google Cloud Dataprep is a fully managed data preparation service that simplifies the process of cleaning, transforming, and visualizing data for analytics and machine learning. Dataprep empowers data analysts and data engineers to prepare data efficiently, leading to faster insights and improved data quality. Google Cloud Data Studio complements these data services by providing a collaborative and interactive data visualization and reporting platform. Data Studio allows users to create interactive dashboards and reports, share them with stakeholders, and make data-driven decisions. The growth of PaaS offerings within Google Cloud reflects the company's commitment to providing a diverse set of tools and services to support modern application development and data-driven decision-making. These PaaS offerings empower developers, data scientists, and organizations to innovate, scale, and extract value from their data efficiently. By abstracting infrastructure complexities and offering a range of developer-friendly services, Google's PaaS offerings enable businesses to focus on building and deploying applications that drive their success in the cloud-native era.

Chapter 3: Microsoft Azure: Unleashing PaaS Potential

Microsoft Azure, a prominent cloud computing platform, boasts a rich set of Platform as a Service (PaaS) capabilities and features. These offerings empower developers and organizations to build, deploy, and manage applications with ease and efficiency. Azure App Service is a key PaaS offering that allows developers to build and host web applications, APIs, and mobile app backends. It supports multiple programming languages, including .NET, Java, Node.js, Python, and PHP, catering to a diverse developer audience. Azure Functions, a serverless computing service, enables developers to write event-driven code in a serverless environment. It automatically scales and handles infrastructure management, allowing developers to focus solely on writing code to respond to events. Azure Kubernetes Service (AKS) simplifies the deployment and management of containerized applications using Kubernetes. It provides a managed Kubernetes cluster that automates updates and scaling, making container orchestration more accessible. Azure Logic Apps facilitate workflow automation and integration between various services, both within Azure and beyond. Developers can create visual workflows to automate processes and connect to various APIs and systems. Azure Functions, Logic Apps, and Azure App Service can all be used in conjunction to build powerful, serverless applications. Azure SQL Database offers fully managed relational database capabilities, supporting SQL Server workloads in the cloud. It provides high availability, scalability, and built-in intelligence for optimal performance. Azure Cosmos DB is a globally distributed, multi-model database service designed for low-latency, high-availability applications. Developers can choose from various data models, including document, key-value, graph, and column-family, to suit their application's needs. Azure Blob Storage serves as a scalable object storage solution for storing and managing unstructured data, such as documents, images, and videos. It offers features like tiered storage, data replication, and integration with other Azure services. Azure Key Vault enhances security by providing a centralized location to store and manage cryptographic keys, secrets, and certificates. This service helps protect sensitive information and simplify key management tasks. Azure Active Directory (Azure AD) is an identity and access management service that enables single sign-on (SSO) and multi-factor authentication (MFA) for applications and services. It integrates with various SaaS applications and supports secure identity management. Azure DevOps, formerly known as Visual Studio Team Services (VSTS), provides a comprehensive set of tools for DevOps practices. It offers version control, build automation, release management, and application monitoring in a single platform. Azure DevTest Labs is a service that helps development and testing teams create and manage environments in the cloud. It offers self-service provisioning, cost management, and integration with Azure DevOps. Azure Monitor and Azure Application Insights offer robust monitoring and diagnostics capabilities for applications and infrastructure. They provide insights into application performance, health, and usage. Azure Site Recovery is a disaster recovery service that ensures business continuity by replicating on-premises workloads to Azure. It enables rapid failover and failback in the event of a disaster. Azure Functions, Logic Apps, and Azure Automation allow organizations to create and automate workflows, helping streamline business processes. Azure Service Fabric provides a microservices platform for building highly scalable and reliable applications. It simplifies the deployment and management of microservices-based applications. Azure Container Instances (ACI) offers a serverless container service that simplifies the deployment of containers without managing the underlying infrastructure. It is ideal for short-lived containerized tasks and microservices. Azure Functions for Kubernetes (KEDA) allows developers to use Azure Functions to autoscale any container in a Kubernetes environment. It extends the capabilities of serverless computing to Kubernetes clusters. Azure Sphere is a comprehensive IoT security solution that combines hardware, software, and cloud components to secure IoT devices. It helps protect devices from emerging threats and vulnerabilities. Azure Arc enables customers to extend Azure services and management to any infrastructure, including on-premises, multicloud, and edge environments. This provides a unified management experience across diverse environments. Azure offers a wide array of PaaS capabilities and features to cater to the needs of developers, IT professionals, and businesses. Whether it's building web applications, deploying containers, managing databases, or implementing IoT solutions, Azure's PaaS offerings provide the flexibility and scalability required for modern cloud-native development. These services abstract infrastructure complexity, allowing organizations to focus on innovation, agility, and delivering value to their customers. As technology evolves, Microsoft continues to expand and enhance its PaaS portfolio to meet the evolving needs of the cloud computing landscape, making Azure a compelling choice for businesses and developers alike.

Azure Platform as a Service (PaaS) offerings find real-world applications across a multitude of industries, demonstrating their versatility and value. In healthcare, Azure PaaS solutions support electronic health record (EHR) systems that store, manage, and secure patient data. These systems enable healthcare providers to access patient information efficiently, improving patient care and reducing administrative burdens. Telemedicine platforms also leverage Azure PaaS capabilities to deliver remote healthcare services, connecting patients and healthcare professionals seamlessly. The scalability and reliability of Azure PaaS services ensure that telemedicine platforms can handle increased demand, especially during health crises. Financial institutions benefit from Azure PaaS by using it to build and deploy robust, secure, and compliant applications. For example, Azure Logic Apps facilitate automated workflows for financial processes, reducing manual errors and improving operational efficiency. Azure SQL Database provides a scalable and reliable solution for financial data storage and analysis, supporting applications such as online banking and trading platforms. In the e-commerce sector, businesses rely on Azure PaaS offerings to build and maintain online stores. Azure App Service allows companies to develop web applications that can handle high traffic volumes during peak shopping seasons. Azure Functions enable e-commerce platforms to create serverless applications for inventory management, order processing, and customer support. Azure DevOps streamlines the continuous deployment of new features and updates, ensuring a seamless shopping experience for customers. Educational institutions leverage Azure PaaS for e-learning platforms, which have become increasingly essential for remote and hybrid learning environments. Azure DevTest Labs enable educators to create virtual labs and learning environments, providing students with hands-on experience. Azure Functions can be used to automate administrative tasks, while Azure Active Directory ensures secure access for students and faculty. Manufacturing companies employ Azure PaaS to optimize production processes and enhance supply chain management. Azure IoT Hub connects and manages IoT devices, allowing manufacturers to collect real-time data for predictive maintenance and quality control. Azure Machine Learning empowers manufacturers to build predictive models that improve production efficiency and reduce downtime. Retailers use Azure PaaS solutions to create personalized customer experiences both in-store and online. Azure Kubernetes Service (AKS) enables retailers to deploy containerized applications for inventory management and point-of-sale systems. Azure Cognitive Services enhance customer engagement by adding AI-driven capabilities like natural language processing and computer vision to chatbots and virtual assistants. In the gaming industry, Azure PaaS services support the development and operation of online multiplayer games. Game developers use Azure Kubernetes Service (AKS) to host game servers, ensuring low-latency experiences for players around the world. Azure Cosmos DB provides a highly responsive and globally distributed database solution, critical for gaming leaderboards and player profiles. For non-profit organizations, Azure PaaS offerings facilitate mission-critical operations and donor engagement. Azure Logic Apps automate fundraising processes, while Azure Functions help manage volunteers and resources efficiently. Azure Active Directory secures access to sensitive donor data, ensuring compliance with data protection regulations. Government agencies harness Azure PaaS capabilities for digital transformation and citizen services. Azure App Service supports the development of government websites and portals that deliver essential information and services to citizens. Azure Security Center strengthens the security posture of government IT systems, safeguarding sensitive data and critical infrastructure. Media and entertainment companies rely on Azure PaaS services for content creation, distribution, and analytics. Azure Media Services enable the encoding, streaming, and monetization of multimedia content, reaching global audiences. Azure Data Lake Storage facilitates content analysis and recommendation engines, enhancing user experiences. Azure PaaS offerings play a pivotal role in the energy sector, supporting the monitoring and management of critical infrastructure. Azure IoT solutions collect data from sensors and devices in the field, enabling predictive maintenance and optimizing energy production. Azure Machine Learning helps energy companies forecast demand, manage resources efficiently, and explore renewable energy solutions. Transportation and logistics companies benefit from Azure PaaS for route optimization, fleet management, and supply chain visibility. Azure

Functions enable the automation of logistics processes, while Azure Maps provide location-based services for delivery tracking and navigation. Azure Synapse Analytics handles massive datasets, aiding in demand forecasting and logistics planning. The entertainment industry utilizes Azure PaaS solutions to create and deliver immersive experiences. Azure Virtual Machines power rendering farms for computer-generated imagery (CGI) and special effects. Azure Media Services enable content streaming for live events, concerts, and sporting matches, reaching a global audience. These real-world applications illustrate the breadth and depth of Azure PaaS offerings across various industries. Azure empowers organizations to innovate, scale, and enhance their operations while benefiting from the flexibility, security, and reliability of the Azure cloud platform. As industries continue to evolve, Azure PaaS remains a valuable tool for addressing complex challenges and driving digital transformation.

Chapter 4: Navigating IBM Cloud's PaaS Ecosystem

IBM Cloud offers a robust suite of Platform as a Service (PaaS) services that cater to the needs of developers, businesses, and enterprises. These PaaS offerings provide a flexible and scalable environment for developing, deploying, and managing applications in the cloud. IBM Cloud Foundry, a powerful PaaS platform, simplifies the deployment and management of cloud-native applications. Developers can leverage Cloud Foundry to build and run applications in various programming languages, including Java, Node.js, and Python. IBM Kubernetes Service (IKS) is a managed Kubernetes platform that facilitates container orchestration and application scaling. IKS streamlines the deployment of containerized applications and offers advanced features for managing Kubernetes clusters. IBM Cloud Functions is a serverless computing service that allows developers to write event-driven code without the need to manage infrastructure. This serverless platform automatically scales and handles resource provisioning based on workload demand. IBM Cloud Code Engine extends the serverless concept to containerized applications, providing a serverless environment for deploying and managing container workloads without the complexity of infrastructure management. IBM Cloud Databases offer a variety of fully managed, scalable database solutions, including IBM Db2, MongoDB, and PostgreSQL. These databases provide high availability, automatic backups, and built-in security features. IBM Cloud Object Storage is an enterprise-grade object storage service designed for storing and managing unstructured data at scale. It offers a cost-effective and reliable solution for storing files, images, and multimedia content. IBM Key Protect enhances security by providing a centralized location to manage encryption keys, secrets, and certificates. This service helps protect sensitive data and simplifies key management tasks. IBM Cloud Identity and Access Management (IAM) is a critical component of IBM Cloud's security model, allowing users to control access to resources and data. It offers fine-grained access control, auditing, and monitoring capabilities to enhance security. IBM Cloud Monitoring and Observability services provide comprehensive insights into the performance and health of applications and infrastructure. These services offer real-time monitoring, alerting, and logging to help operators and developers troubleshoot and optimize their environments. IBM Cloud Security and Compliance Center (CSCC) provides security risk and compliance management across IBM Cloud resources. It helps organizations maintain compliance with industry-specific regulations and security standards. IBM Cloud for VMware Solutions offers a dedicated cloud infrastructure for running VMware workloads in the cloud. This solution enables seamless workload migration and provides a consistent operational experience for VMware environments. IBM Cloud Automation Manager simplifies the deployment and management of multi-cloud and hybrid cloud environments. It enables automated provisioning and scaling of resources across various cloud platforms. IBM Cloud Pak for Applications provides a comprehensive development and management platform for building, deploying, and modernizing applications. It supports microservices architectures, containerization, and DevOps practices. IBM Cloud Pak for Multicloud Management offers a unified management solution for multi-cloud environments, providing visibility and control across different cloud providers. IBM Cloud Pak for Integration streamlines the integration of applications and data across hybrid and multi-cloud environments. It supports API management, event-driven architecture, and data integration. IBM Cloud Pak for Data empowers organizations to collect, organize, and analyze data across hybrid and multi-cloud environments. It offers advanced data analytics, machine learning, and data governance capabilities. IBM Cloud Pak for Watson AIOps leverages AI and machine learning to enhance IT operations and automate incident resolution. It helps organizations proactively manage and optimize their IT infrastructure. IBM Cloud Pak for Security provides a unified security platform that helps organizations detect and respond to security threats across their cloud and on-premises environments. IBM Cloud Pak for Network Automation enables the automation and orchestration of network services in multi-cloud and hybrid cloud environments. It simplifies network management and enhances agility. IBM Cloud Satellite extends the IBM Cloud to edge locations and on-premises environments, allowing organizations to run cloud-native workloads wherever they need them. These PaaS offerings demonstrate the breadth and depth of IBM Cloud's capabilities for modern application development, data management, and hybrid cloud solutions. Whether it's building cloud-native applications, managing data, ensuring security and compliance, or automating infrastructure, IBM Cloud PaaS services provide the tools and flexibility organizations need to drive innovation and meet their business goals. As technology continues to evolve, IBM Cloud remains committed to expanding and enhancing its PaaS portfolio to address the evolving needs of the cloud computing landscape, making it a compelling choice for businesses and developers alike. Implementing Platform as a Service (PaaS) solutions from IBM Cloud has led to numerous success stories across various industries. One compelling case study comes from a leading e-commerce company that sought to modernize its online platform. By utilizing IBM Cloud PaaS offerings, the company was able to build and deploy containerized microservices that improved the performance and scalability of its e-commerce website. The flexibility of IBM Kubernetes Service (IKS) allowed the company to seamlessly manage its containerized workloads, ensuring high availability and rapid response to traffic spikes. In the healthcare sector, a large hospital network embarked on a digital transformation journey to enhance patient care and streamline operations. IBM Cloud Foundry provided the ideal platform for developing and deploying healthcare applications that integrated seamlessly with the hospital's existing systems. This PaaS solution allowed the hospital to accelerate the development of patient portals, electronic health records, and telehealth services. A global financial institution faced the challenge of modernizing its legacy applications while ensuring security and compliance. By leveraging IBM Cloud Pak for Applications, the institution successfully refactored its monolithic applications into microservices-based architectures. This transformation improved application agility and reduced development time, enabling the institution to respond more swiftly to market demands. An educational institution embracing online learning experienced a surge in demand for its e-learning platform. To meet this increased demand, the institution adopted IBM Cloud Functions to create serverless functions that could automatically scale in response to user activity. This serverless approach ensured a seamless and responsive learning experience for students. A manufacturing company operating across multiple geographies sought to optimize its supply chain and production processes. IBM Cloud Pak for Integration facilitated the integration of disparate systems and data sources, enabling real-time visibility into supply chain operations. As a result, the company achieved cost savings and efficiency gains across its global manufacturing network. In the entertainment industry, a major media company faced the challenge of rapidly processing and delivering content to a global audience. IBM Cloud's serverless capabilities, including IBM Cloud Functions and IBM Cloud Object Storage, enabled the company to build a scalable and efficient content distribution pipeline. This solution ensured low-latency content delivery to viewers worldwide. For a government agency responsible for citizen services, security and compliance were paramount. IBM Cloud Security and Compliance Center (CSCC) provided the agency with a centralized platform to monitor and manage security across its cloud resources. This comprehensive solution helped the agency maintain compliance with regulatory requirements. A transportation and logistics company sought to optimize its fleet management and route planning. IBM Cloud Pak for Multicloud Management provided the company with a unified platform for managing its multi-cloud environments. This solution improved visibility into operations, enhanced resource utilization, and reduced operational costs. In the energy sector, an organization operating critical infrastructure needed to monitor and maintain its equipment efficiently. IBM Cloud for VMware Solutions allowed the organization to extend its on-premises VMware environment to the cloud seamlessly. This hybrid cloud approach improved resource utilization and ensured the availability of critical services. In the retail industry, a global e-commerce platform needed to enhance its customer experience and support high traffic volumes. IBM Cloud's serverless capabilities, such as IBM Cloud Functions and IBM Cloud Code Engine, allowed the platform to build responsive and scalable applications. This resulted in improved customer satisfaction and increased sales. These case studies highlight the diverse applications of IBM Cloud PaaS offerings across various industries. From e-commerce and healthcare to finance and education, organizations have successfully leveraged IBM Cloud PaaS solutions to address their unique challenges and drive innovation. These success stories underscore the adaptability and value of PaaS in enabling organizations to modernize their applications, enhance customer experiences, and streamline operations. As technology continues to evolve, IBM Cloud remains at the forefront of delivering flexible and scalable PaaS solutions to meet the dynamic needs of businesses across the globe.

Chapter 5: Selecting the Right PaaS Solution for Your Needs

Assessing your business requirements is a critical step in any decision-making process, particularly when it comes to technology investments. Before you embark on a journey to implement new solutions or make significant changes to your existing systems, it's essential to thoroughly understand what your business truly needs. The first key consideration in assessing your business requirements is to define your objectives and goals. What are you trying to achieve with this investment or change in your operations? Are you looking to increase efficiency, reduce costs, improve customer service, or enter new markets? Defining clear and specific objectives will provide a solid foundation for evaluating potential solutions. Next, you should consider the unique characteristics and challenges of your industry. Every industry has its own set of regulations, standards, and best practices that can impact the technology solutions you choose. Understanding these industry-specific requirements is crucial to ensure compliance and competitiveness. Another critical aspect of assessing your business requirements is understanding your current technology infrastructure. What systems and applications are already in place, and how do they support your operations? Identifying any existing gaps or limitations in your technology stack is essential to determine what needs improvement or integration. It's also essential to involve key stakeholders in the assessment process. Engage with employees, department heads, and management to gather insights into their pain points and needs. Their input can provide valuable perspectives on how technology can better support their daily tasks and overall objectives. Consider the scalability of your business as well. Think about how your requirements might evolve in the future. Choosing a solution that can grow with your business can save you from costly and disruptive technology migrations down the road. Budget considerations play a significant role in assessing your business requirements. You need to have a clear understanding of your budget constraints and how much you can allocate to technology investments. This will help you determine the feasibility of different solutions and whether they align with your financial resources. Additionally, it's crucial to evaluate the potential return on investment (ROI) for any technology solution you're considering. What benefits do you expect to gain, and when can you reasonably expect to see a return on your investment? A well-defined ROI analysis can provide a compelling case for moving forward with a particular solution. Consider the potential impact on your workforce. Will the new technology require additional training or changes in job roles? Understanding how your employees will adapt to the changes is essential for a smooth transition and successful implementation. Security and data protection are paramount in today's digital landscape. Assess your business requirements in terms of cybersecurity and compliance with data privacy regulations. Make sure that any technology solutions you consider align with your security and compliance needs. Evaluate the technical expertise within your organization. Do you have in-house IT teams with the skills necessary to implement and maintain the chosen solution, or will you require external support? Assess the availability of resources, both human and technical, for successful implementation. Consider the user experience (UX) and how the new technology will impact your customers or clients. Will it enhance their experience or potentially create challenges? A seamless and user-friendly solution is more likely to meet your business requirements effectively. Finally, assess the competitive landscape. What are your competitors doing in terms of technology adoption? Understanding how technology is shaping your industry can help you stay ahead or at least keep pace with market trends. In summary, assessing your business requirements is a multifaceted process that involves understanding your objectives, industry-specific needs, current infrastructure, stakeholder input, scalability, budget, ROI, workforce impact, security and compliance, technical expertise, resource availability, user experience, and competitive landscape. Taking a comprehensive approach to this assessment will enable you to make informed decisions that align with your business's goals and position you for success in an ever-evolving technological landscape. A comparative analysis of Platform as a Service (PaaS) providers is a crucial step for businesses and developers seeking the right cloud platform for their specific needs. PaaS solutions offer a range of services, tools, and infrastructure to support application development and deployment. Among the major PaaS providers, such as Amazon Web Services (AWS), Microsoft Azure, Google Cloud Platform (GCP), IBM Cloud, and others, there are both similarities and differences that can significantly impact your choice. One key factor in this analysis is the range of programming languages and frameworks supported by each provider. AWS Elastic Beanstalk, for example, offers support for multiple languages, including Java, .NET, Node.js, Python, Ruby, and PHP, providing developers with flexibility. Similarly, Microsoft Azure App Service supports popular languages like .NET, Java, Node.js, Python, and PHP, making it versatile for a wide range of applications. Google App Engine, on the other hand, specializes in Python, Java, PHP, Node.js, Ruby, and Go, while IBM Cloud Foundry supports multiple languages, including Java, Node.js, Ruby, and Go. Another aspect to consider is the scalability and performance of the PaaS provider. AWS Elastic Beanstalk and Azure App Service offer automatic scaling to handle increased traffic, making them suitable for applications with varying workloads. GCP's App Engine also offers automatic scaling, ensuring applications can handle changes in demand efficiently. IBM Cloud Foundry provides scaling capabilities, but the level of automation may require more manual intervention. Database services are a critical consideration in PaaS selection. AWS offers Amazon RDS (Relational Database Service) and Amazon DynamoDB for both relational and NoSQL databases. Azure provides Azure SQL Database and Azure Cosmos DB, catering to relational and NoSQL database needs. Google Cloud offers Cloud SQL for relational databases and Cloud Datastore for NoSQL databases. IBM Cloud provides services like Db2 and Cloudant to address various database requirements. Integration with other cloud services and tools is vital for seamless development and deployment. AWS offers a wide range of integrated services, including AWS Lambda for serverless computing, AWS CodeDeploy for automated deployments, and AWS CodePipeline for continuous integration and continuous delivery (CI/CD). Azure provides Azure Functions for serverless computing, Azure DevOps for CI/CD, and Azure Logic Apps for workflow automation. GCP offers Cloud Functions for serverless computing and Cloud Build for CI/CD pipelines. IBM Cloud provides integration with services like IBM Cloud Functions and Jenkins for CI/CD. Pricing is a significant factor in choosing a PaaS provider. AWS, Azure, GCP, and IBM Cloud all offer pricing models that can be complex due to the variety of services and resources available. Understanding your specific usage patterns and requirements is essential to accurately estimate costs. Security and compliance are paramount in cloud computing. AWS, Azure, GCP, and IBM Cloud all provide robust security features, including identity and access management (IAM), encryption, and compliance certifications. It's essential to evaluate each provider's security offerings to ensure they align with your organization's requirements. Support and documentation play a crucial role in the developer experience. AWS, Azure, GCP, and IBM Cloud offer extensive documentation, tutorials, and support options. Consider the availability and quality of support when *making your decision. Community and ecosystem are factors to consider as well. AWS, Azure, GCP, and IBM Cloud have large developer communities and ecosystems with a wealth of third-party tools and integrations. Evaluate how well each provider's ecosystem aligns with your project's needs. Vendor lock-in is a potential concern when choosing a PaaS provider. AWS, Azure, GCP, and IBM Cloud all have proprietary services and technologies. Consider the portability of your applications and data when assessing vendor lock-in risks. Geographical presence and data center locations can impact latency and data sovereignty. AWS, Azure, GCP, and IBM Cloud have global data center networks. Consider the geographical regions where each provider has a presence and how it aligns with your target audience and compliance requirements. In summary, a comparative analysis of PaaS providers involves evaluating factors such as language support, scalability, database services, integration, pricing, security, support, documentation, community, vendor lock-in, and geographical presence. Each of the major PaaS providers offers a unique set of services and capabilities, and the choice ultimately depends on your specific project requirements and organizational needs. By carefully assessing these factors and conducting a thorough analysis, you can make an informed decision that aligns with your goals and sets you on a path toward successful application development and deployment in the cloud.*

Chapter 6: Building and Deploying PaaS Applications

The Platform as a Service (PaaS) application development workflow encompasses a series of steps that guide developers from initial concept to the deployment and management of a cloud-native application. At its core, PaaS aims to streamline and simplify the development process, allowing developers to focus on coding and innovation rather than managing infrastructure. The first phase of the PaaS application development workflow involves ideation and planning. During this stage, developers, product managers, and stakeholders collaborate to define the objectives, features, and scope of the application. This phase often includes brainstorming sessions, requirement gathering, and the creation of a project roadmap. Once the project's goals are clear, developers move on to the design and architecture phase. Here, they create the application's architecture, data models, and user interfaces. The choice of programming languages, frameworks, and databases plays a critical role in shaping the application's design. Developers also consider scalability, security, and user experience during this phase. With a solid design in place, developers proceed to the actual coding phase. They write the application's code, following best practices and coding standards. PaaS platforms typically provide development tools and integrated development environments (IDEs) that facilitate coding and debugging. Collaboration among team members is essential during this phase to ensure that the codebase aligns with the project's goals. As coding progresses, developers often conduct code reviews and testing to catch and address issues early. Continuous integration and continuous delivery (CI/CD) pipelines are established to automate the building, testing, and deployment of code changes. Once the initial coding is complete, developers focus on testing and quality assurance. They perform various types of testing, including unit testing, integration testing, and user acceptance testing, to identify and rectify bugs and issues. PaaS platforms offer testing and debugging tools that streamline this process. Test-driven development (TDD) and automated testing frameworks are commonly used practices to maintain code quality. Security is a crucial consideration throughout the development workflow. Developers implement security measures such as data encryption, authentication, and authorization to protect the application and its data. PaaS providers often offer security features and services to help developers secure their applications effectively. Once the application is thoroughly tested and meets the required quality standards, it's time to prepare for deployment. PaaS platforms simplify the deployment process by providing tools and services for packaging and containerizing applications. Developers can define deployment configurations, including resource allocation, environment variables, and scaling rules. PaaS providers also offer deployment options, such as rolling deployments and blue-green deployments, to minimize downtime and ensure reliability. With the application successfully deployed, developers shift their focus to monitoring and management. PaaS platforms offer monitoring and observability tools that provide insights into application performance, resource utilization, and error tracking. Developers set up alerts and notifications to proactively address issues and optimize application performance. Scaling is an integral part of the management phase. Developers can configure auto-scaling rules to ensure that the application can handle changes in workload and traffic. This dynamic scaling helps maintain optimal performance and cost-efficiency. Security remains a continuous concern in the management phase. Developers regularly apply security patches, update dependencies, and conduct security assessments to protect against emerging threats. Data management is another critical aspect of PaaS application management. Developers utilize database services provided by the PaaS platform to store, retrieve, and manage data efficiently. Regular backups and disaster recovery planning are essential components of data management. In addition to monitoring, scaling, security, and data management, developers also focus on continuous improvement. They collect feedback from users, analyze application performance metrics, and identify areas for enhancement. PaaS platforms support iterative development, enabling developers to make incremental improvements to the application over time. Collaboration and communication remain crucial throughout the entire PaaS application development workflow. Effective communication ensures that all team members, including developers, testers, and operations staff, are aligned with project goals and priorities. Collaboration tools and version control systems facilitate teamwork and code management. Documentation is essential to capture architectural decisions, coding guidelines, and operational procedures.

PaaS platforms often provide documentation templates and integration with documentation tools to simplify this process. In summary, the PaaS application development workflow consists of several interconnected phases, including ideation and planning, design and architecture, coding, testing and quality assurance, deployment, monitoring and management, and continuous improvement. Throughout this workflow, developers leverage PaaS platforms to streamline and automate various aspects of application development and maintenance. Effective collaboration, security, and communication are essential elements that contribute to the successful development and operation of cloud-native applications in a PaaS environment. Deployment strategies for Platform as a Service (PaaS) environments play a pivotal role in the successful delivery of applications and services in the cloud. These strategies encompass a range of approaches, methodologies, and best practices that help organizations deploy their software efficiently, securely, and reliably. One common deployment strategy is the Blue-Green deployment, which involves maintaining two identical production environments, one referred to as "Blue" and the other as "Green." In this approach, the Blue environment hosts the current version of the application, while the Green environment remains inactive. When it's time to deploy a new version of the application, the update is first deployed to the Green environment. Testing and validation are performed in the Green environment to ensure the new version functions correctly. Once the new version is deemed stable and reliable, traffic is switched from the Blue environment to the Green environment, making it the new production environment. The Blue environment now becomes the inactive one, ready to host the next deployment. This strategy minimizes downtime and allows for easy rollback to the previous version if issues arise during deployment. Canary deployment is another strategy that enables organizations to roll out new features or updates gradually. In a Canary deployment, a small subset of users or traffic is directed to the new version of the application, while the majority of users continue to use the existing version. This approach allows organizations to gather real-world feedback and monitor the performance and stability of the new version in a controlled manner. If any issues or anomalies are detected, they can be addressed before rolling out the new version to a broader audience. Canary deployments are particularly useful for organizations that prioritize cautious and data-driven release processes. Feature toggles, also known as feature flags or feature switches, are a deployment strategy that allows developers to enable or disable specific features within an application at runtime. Feature toggles are often used in conjunction with continuous integration and continuous deployment (CI/CD) pipelines. By using feature toggles, organizations can deploy new code to production while keeping certain features hidden from users until they are fully tested and ready to be released. This approach provides a high degree of control and flexibility over the deployment process. A/B testing is a deployment strategy that involves exposing different versions of an application or feature to different groups of users and measuring their preferences and behavior. A/B testing is commonly used in marketing and user experience optimization, but it can also be applied to *software deployment. By comparing the performance and user engagement metrics of different versions, organizations can make data-driven decisions about which version to deploy to a broader audience. A/B testing helps organizations ensure that new features or changes resonate with users and meet their needs. Rolling deployments are a strategy where new versions of an application are gradually deployed to subsets of servers or instances within an environment. This approach reduces the risk of potential issues affecting the entire environment. Each subset of servers is updated one at a time, and the deployment progresses incrementally. Rolling deployments can be particularly useful for large-scale applications with multiple servers or instances. Serverless deployment, also known as Function as a Service (FaaS), is a deployment strategy that abstracts server management entirely. In a serverless deployment, developers focus on writing code in the form of functions or microservices, and the cloud provider handles the underlying infrastructure. This approach offers high scalability, cost-efficiency, and automatic scaling based on demand. Serverless deployment is suitable for applications with variable workloads and event-driven architectures. Immutable deployments involve replacing the entire application environment with each new deployment. Instead of updating or modifying existing servers or instances, immutable deployments create new, fresh instances that include the latest code and configuration. This strategy eliminates the risk of configuration drift and ensures consistency across deployments. Organizations adopting immutable deployments often use infrastructure as code (IaC) to automate the provisioning of new instances. Hybrid deployment strategies combine multiple deployment approaches to meet specific requirements. For example, an organization may use Canary deployments for its web application while adopting a serverless approach for processing background tasks or handling specific functions. Hybrid deployments offer flexibility and can be tailored to the unique needs of the application and organization. In summary, deployment strategies for PaaS environments are essential for delivering applications and updates efficiently, reliably, and with minimal disruption. The choice of deployment strategy depends on factors such as the organization's risk tolerance, the complexity of the application, the need for gradual rollout, and the desire for real-time feedback from users. By selecting and implementing the right deployment strategy, organizations can optimize their deployment processes and deliver high-quality software to users and customers.*

Chapter 7: Advanced PaaS Development Techniques

Leveraging containers in Platform as a Service (PaaS) environments has become a fundamental practice for modern application development and deployment. Containers are lightweight, portable, and offer a consistent environment for running applications, making them an ideal choice for PaaS platforms. Containers encapsulate an application and its dependencies, including libraries and runtime, into a single unit. This encapsulation ensures that the application can run consistently across different environments, from development to production. One of the most popular containerization technologies is Docker, which provides a standard format for packaging applications and their dependencies. PaaS platforms often include native support for Docker containers, simplifying the deployment and management of containerized applications. Containers provide isolation, enabling multiple applications to run on the same host without interfering with each other. This isolation ensures that each application has its own runtime environment, reducing conflicts and dependencies. Containers are highly efficient in terms of resource utilization, as they share the host operating system's kernel while maintaining separate user spaces. This efficiency results in faster startup times and lower overhead compared to traditional virtual machines (VMs). Containers offer excellent scalability, allowing organizations to scale their applications horizontally by adding more containers as needed. PaaS platforms can automatically manage container scaling based on traffic and workload demand. Containers facilitate version control and reproducibility. Developers can package their applications into containers, including all dependencies and configurations, ensuring that the application behaves consistently across different environments. Versioning and rollback become more manageable with containers, as previous versions can be preserved and deployed as needed. Containers support microservices architectures, where applications are composed of small, loosely coupled services. Each microservice can be containerized independently, enabling teams to develop, deploy, and scale individual services without affecting the entire application. This modularity enhances agility and flexibility in application development. Containers are portable, allowing applications to run seamlessly across different PaaS environments and cloud providers. Developers can build once and deploy anywhere, reducing vendor lock-in and facilitating multi-cloud strategies. Containers can be orchestrated and managed using container orchestration platforms like Kubernetes. Kubernetes automates the deployment, scaling, and management of containerized applications, making it an integral part of many PaaS offerings. Kubernetes provides features such as load balancing, self-healing, and rolling updates, enhancing the resilience and availability of containerized applications. PaaS platforms that incorporate Kubernetes offer developers a powerful toolset for managing container workloads. Containers support the concept of immutable infrastructure, where infrastructure components are treated as disposable and replaceable. This approach simplifies updates and maintenance, as new containers are created to replace outdated ones rather than patching existing infrastructure. Security is a critical consideration when leveraging containers in PaaS environments. Containers should be built with security best practices in mind, including regular security scans and vulnerability assessments. Container runtimes should be configured to minimize attack surfaces and follow security guidelines. Container images should be signed and verified to ensure their authenticity. PaaS platforms often provide security features and integrations to enhance container security. DevOps practices and CI/CD pipelines are closely associated with containerization in PaaS environments. Developers can integrate containerization into their CI/CD workflows to automate the building, testing, and deployment of container images. Container registries store and distribute container images, making them accessible to development and deployment pipelines. Continuous integration helps catch issues early in the development process, ensuring that containerized applications are reliable and performant. Monitoring and observability are essential when using containers in PaaS environments. Container orchestration platforms like Kubernetes offer built-in monitoring and logging capabilities. Developers and operators can gain insights into container performance, resource utilization, and application behavior. Alerting and notification systems can proactively detect and address issues within containerized applications. Containerization has become a standard practice for organizations adopting PaaS solutions. It enables a more efficient, scalable, and modular approach to application development and deployment. By embracing containers, organizations can benefit from improved resource utilization, enhanced agility, simplified management, and increased portability across different PaaS environments. Containers, coupled with container orchestration and DevOps practices, have become instrumental in modernizing IT operations and accelerating the delivery of software applications. Microservices architecture has emerged as a powerful approach to building and deploying applications in Platform as a Service (PaaS) environments. This architectural style breaks down complex applications into smaller, independently deployable services that work together to deliver functionality. In a microservices architecture, each service focuses on a specific business capability, and these services communicate through APIs or other lightweight mechanisms. This approach provides several advantages for organizations leveraging PaaS platforms. One of the key benefits of microservices architecture in PaaS is agility. Microservices enable organizations to develop, deploy, and scale individual services independently, reducing the complexity of managing monolithic applications. This agility allows for faster development cycles and the ability to respond quickly to changing business requirements. Another advantage is scalability.

Microservices can be scaled independently based on workload demand, ensuring that resources are allocated efficiently. This scalability is especially valuable for applications with varying usage patterns or seasonal spikes in traffic. Microservices promote modularity, making it easier to build, test, and maintain each service in isolation. Development teams can focus on specific services, leading to improved productivity and code quality. This modularity also facilitates code reuse, as services can be shared across different applications or projects. Microservices architecture enhances fault tolerance and resilience. When one service experiences an issue or failure, it doesn't necessarily affect the entire application. Redundancy and load balancing can be implemented at the service level, ensuring that services remain available even in the face of failures. Continuous integration and continuous deployment (CI/CD) pipelines are a natural fit for microservices. Each service can have its own CI/CD pipeline, enabling automated testing, building, and deployment. This automation streamlines the release process and ensures that changes can be deployed quickly and reliably. Microservices can be developed using different programming languages and frameworks, allowing organizations to choose the technology that best suits each service's requirements. This flexibility enables the use of specialized languages or tools for specific tasks, such as machine learning, data processing, or real-time analytics. Microservices also align well with containerization. Each service can be packaged as a container, providing consistency in deployment across different environments. Container orchestration platforms like Kubernetes simplify the management and scaling of microservices. Service discovery and load balancing are critical aspects of microservices architecture. PaaS platforms often provide built-in solutions for service discovery and load balancing, ensuring that requests are routed to the appropriate service instances. API gateways are commonly used to manage and expose APIs for microservices. These gateways centralize API management, allowing for authentication, rate limiting, and request transformation. Security is a paramount concern when implementing microservices. Each service should be secured independently, and PaaS platforms offer security features such as identity and access management, encryption, and compliance certifications. Monitoring and observability are crucial for gaining insights into the performance and behavior of microservices. PaaS platforms often provide monitoring and logging tools to track metrics, troubleshoot issues, and ensure that services meet their service-level objectives (SLOs). Challenges also accompany microservices architecture in PaaS environments. One of the main challenges is managing the complexity of numerous services. As the number of services grows, organizations must implement effective governance, documentation, and communication strategies. Testing can become more complex in a microservices ecosystem. End-to-end testing may require orchestrating interactions between multiple services, and organizations may need to invest in testing frameworks and tools that support microservices testing. Service dependencies and versioning require careful consideration. Changes to one service may impact services that rely on it, necessitating a well-defined versioning strategy and compatibility checks. Monitoring and troubleshooting can be challenging in a distributed microservices environment. Organizations must invest in robust observability solutions to gain visibility into the entire system. Cultural changes may be necessary to fully embrace microservices. Development teams must adopt a DevOps mindset, taking ownership of the services they develop, deploy, and operate. Effective communication and collaboration among teams are essential for success. In summary, microservices architecture is a powerful approach for building and deploying applications in PaaS environments. It offers agility, scalability, modularity, fault tolerance, and flexibility, making it well-suited for modern application development. While challenges exist, organizations that invest in the right tools, practices, and cultural changes can harness the benefits of microservices architecture to deliver innovative and resilient applications in PaaS.

Chapter 8: PaaS and Hybrid Cloud Strategies

Strategies for combining on-premises and cloud Platform as a Service (PaaS) environments are crucial for organizations seeking to leverage the benefits of both worlds. Hybrid cloud solutions that integrate on-premises infrastructure with cloud-based PaaS offerings provide flexibility, scalability, and cost-efficiency. One strategy for combining on-premises and cloud PaaS involves adopting a hybrid cloud architecture. In this approach, certain workloads or services are hosted on-premises, while others run in the cloud. Organizations can choose to move specific workloads to the cloud, such as development and testing environments, web applications, or data analytics, while keeping mission-critical or sensitive workloads on-premises. This flexibility allows organizations to align their infrastructure with their unique requirements and compliance needs. A key aspect of a successful hybrid cloud strategy is seamless connectivity and networking between on-premises and cloud environments. Organizations can establish secure and high-performance connections, such as dedicated network links or virtual private networks (VPNs), to ensure data and application traffic flow efficiently between the two environments. Integration is a critical component of combining on-premises and cloud PaaS. Organizations need to ensure that on-premises and cloud applications can communicate and share data seamlessly.

Integration platforms and middleware solutions can facilitate the exchange of data and services between environments, enabling real-time information flow. Data synchronization and replication tools can keep data consistent across on-premises and cloud databases. Identity and access management (IAM) is essential for maintaining security and compliance. Organizations should implement unified IAM solutions that manage user identities and access rights consistently across on-premises and cloud environments. This ensures that users have secure and controlled access to resources, regardless of where they are hosted. Security is a paramount concern when combining on-premises and cloud PaaS. Organizations should implement a comprehensive security strategy that covers both environments. This strategy includes data encryption, access controls, threat detection, and vulnerability assessments. Organizations must also stay vigilant about security updates and patches in both on-premises and cloud environments. A disaster recovery and business continuity strategy is crucial to protect against data loss and downtime. Organizations should create backup and recovery plans that encompass both on-premises and cloud resources. This ensures that critical data and applications can be quickly restored in the event of an outage or disaster. Cost management is another consideration in combining on-premises and cloud PaaS. Organizations should monitor and optimize their cloud spending to avoid unexpected costs. This may involve rightsizing cloud resources, leveraging reserved instances, and using cost management tools provided by cloud providers. Automation plays a significant role in managing hybrid cloud environments. Organizations can use automation tools and scripts to provision, configure, and manage resources consistently across on-premises and cloud environments. Automation enhances efficiency and reduces the risk of human errors. Performance monitoring and optimization are ongoing tasks in hybrid cloud environments. Organizations should use monitoring and analytics tools to gain insights into the performance of on-premises and cloud resources. These insights can help identify bottlenecks, optimize resource allocation, and ensure that workloads perform at their best. Scalability is a significant advantage of combining on-premises and cloud PaaS. Organizations can leverage cloud resources to handle spikes in demand while keeping baseline workloads on-premises. This scalability ensures that applications remain responsive and cost-effective. Multi-cloud strategies involve using multiple cloud providers to diversify risk and take advantage of unique features. Organizations combining on-premises and cloud PaaS can also explore multi-cloud approaches, where different workloads are hosted on different cloud platforms to maximize benefits. Containerization and orchestration technologies like Docker and Kubernetes can facilitate workload portability across on-premises and cloud environments. Organizations can package applications in containers and deploy them consistently in both environments. This approach simplifies the movement of workloads and ensures consistency. Hybrid cloud management platforms provide centralized control and visibility into hybrid environments. These platforms offer tools for managing resources, monitoring performance, and optimizing costs across on-premises and cloud PaaS. Choosing the right hybrid cloud management platform can streamline operations and improve overall efficiency. In summary, strategies for combining on-premises and cloud PaaS environments require careful planning and execution. Organizations should consider hybrid cloud architectures, connectivity, integration, security, IAM, disaster recovery, cost management, automation, performance monitoring, scalability, multi-cloud approaches, containerization, and hybrid cloud management platforms. By adopting a holistic approach to hybrid cloud, organizations can harness the benefits of both on-premises and cloud PaaS to drive innovation and growth while maintaining control and security. Hybrid cloud solutions have gained significant traction in recent years, offering organizations the ability to combine the benefits of on-premises and cloud environments. These solutions provide a versatile platform for various use cases, enabling organizations to meet specific business needs while optimizing their IT infrastructure. One common hybrid cloud use case is workload flexibility. Organizations can leverage on-premises resources for stable and predictable workloads while using the cloud for burst capacity during periods of increased demand. This approach ensures that applications remain responsive without overprovisioning on-premises infrastructure. Another use case is data backup and disaster recovery. Hybrid cloud allows organizations to store critical data both on-premises and in the cloud, providing redundancy and resilience. In the event of a disaster or data loss, organizations can quickly recover from the cloud, minimizing downtime and data loss. Hybrid cloud also supports data archiving. Organizations can offload infrequently accessed data to cost-effective cloud storage while keeping frequently accessed data on-premises. This approach optimizes storage costs while maintaining data accessibility. A popular use case for hybrid cloud is application development and testing. Developers can use cloud resources to provision development and testing environments quickly, taking advantage of the cloud's scalability and agility. Once testing is complete, applications can be deployed on-premises or in the cloud, depending on production requirements. Hybrid cloud supports geographic redundancy for high availability. Organizations can deploy applications in multiple geographic regions, ensuring uninterrupted service in the event of regional outages or disruptions. This redundancy enhances business continuity and minimizes service interruptions. Hybrid cloud is well-suited for compliance and regulatory requirements. Organizations subject to data sovereignty or industry-specific regulations can store sensitive data on-premises while using the cloud for non-sensitive workloads. This separation ensures compliance while taking advantage of cloud capabilities. Hybrid cloud facilitates data migration and synchronization. Organizations can use cloud services to replicate data between on-premises and cloud environments, ensuring that data is always *up-to-date and accessible from either location. This use case is valuable for global organizations with distributed data needs. Hybrid cloud also supports the Internet of Things (IoT). Organizations can process and analyze IoT data in the cloud while maintaining local processing for critical real-time applications on-premises. This approach balances scalability and latency requirements. Best practices for successful hybrid cloud implementations start with a clear understanding of business objectives and IT requirements. Organizations should identify which workloads and data are suitable for the cloud and which should remain on-premises. A well-defined hybrid cloud strategy aligns IT decisions with business goals. Effective connectivity and networking are essential for hybrid cloud success. Organizations should establish secure and high-performance connections between on-premises and cloud environments. This connectivity ensures efficient data transfer and seamless communication between resources. Integration is a critical aspect of hybrid cloud. Organizations must ensure that on-premises and cloud applications can interact seamlessly. Integration solutions, middleware, and API gateways can facilitate data and service exchange. Data management is a key consideration. Organizations should define data storage, backup, and archiving policies to optimize data placement across on-premises and cloud environments. Effective data synchronization tools and practices are essential to maintain data consistency. Security is paramount in hybrid cloud environments. Organizations must implement robust security measures, including encryption, access controls, and threat detection, to protect data and resources. Identity and access management (IAM) should provide unified control across on-premises and cloud environments. Organizations should prioritize a comprehensive disaster recovery and business continuity plan. This plan should encompass both on-premises and cloud resources to ensure rapid recovery and minimal downtime in the event of disruptions. Cost management is critical in hybrid cloud environments. Organizations should monitor and optimize cloud spending to avoid unexpected costs. Cost allocation and budgeting tools can help track expenses. Automation plays a significant role in hybrid cloud operations. Organizations should automate provisioning, scaling, and management tasks to improve efficiency and reduce manual errors. Performance monitoring and optimization are ongoing responsibilities. Organizations should regularly assess the performance of on-premises and cloud resources, optimizing resource allocation and configurations. Scalability is an advantage of hybrid cloud. Organizations should leverage cloud resources for scalability during peak demand, ensuring that applications remain responsive and cost-effective. Multi-cloud strategies, using multiple cloud providers, can enhance flexibility and resilience. Organizations should consider the use of multiple cloud platforms to diversify risk and access unique features. Containerization and orchestration technologies simplify workload portability between on-premises and cloud environments. Organizations should adopt containerization and orchestration solutions to streamline deployment and management. A hybrid cloud management platform can provide centralized control and visibility. Organizations should explore hybrid cloud management platforms to simplify resource management, monitoring, and governance. In summary, hybrid cloud use cases encompass workload flexibility, data backup and disaster recovery, data archiving, application development and testing, geographic redundancy, compliance, and data migration. Best practices for successful hybrid cloud implementations include aligning with business objectives, establishing effective connectivity, prioritizing integration, optimizing data management, ensuring security, implementing IAM, disaster recovery planning, cost management, automation, performance monitoring, scalability, multi-cloud strategies, containerization, and adopting hybrid cloud management platforms. By following these best practices, organizations can harness the advantages of hybrid cloud to meet their specific business needs while maintaining control and security over their IT infrastructure.*

Chapter 9: Ensuring Security and Compliance in Paas Environments

PaaS security best practices are essential for organizations to protect their cloud-based applications and data. Security is a top concern when deploying applications on PaaS platforms, as they often involve sensitive information and critical business processes. One fundamental aspect of PaaS security is identity and access management (IAM). Organizations should implement strong authentication and authorization mechanisms to ensure that only authorized users and applications can access PaaS resources. Using multi-factor authentication (MFA) adds an extra layer of security by requiring users to provide multiple forms of verification. Role-based access control (RBAC) should be employed to grant permissions based on job roles and responsibilities, limiting access to what is necessary for each user. Regularly reviewing and updating IAM policies is crucial to keep security permissions aligned with organizational changes. Encryption plays a pivotal role in PaaS security. Data should be encrypted both in transit and at rest. Secure Sockets Layer (SSL)/Transport Layer Security (TLS) protocols should be used for data in transit to protect against eavesdropping and man-in-the-middle attacks. Data at rest should be encrypted using strong encryption algorithms. Many PaaS providers offer built-in encryption features, making it easier to implement encryption for databases and storage. Data privacy and compliance are of paramount importance. Organizations should ensure that their PaaS provider complies with relevant data protection regulations and standards, such as GDPR, HIPAA, or PCI DSS, depending on their industry and location. Data classification and data loss prevention (DLP) solutions can help identify and protect sensitive data. Regularly monitoring and auditing access to data is essential to identify any unauthorized or suspicious activities. Security patch management is crucial to protect against known vulnerabilities. PaaS providers typically handle the underlying infrastructure's security, but organizations are responsible for securing their applications and data. Regularly applying security patches and updates to both the operating system and application components is essential to address known vulnerabilities. Vulnerability scanning tools can help identify potential security weaknesses that need attention. Continuous monitoring and incident response are essential components of PaaS security. Security information and event management (SIEM) solutions can provide real-time monitoring of PaaS environments, alerting organizations to any anomalies or security incidents. Organizations should have a well-defined incident response plan in place to address security breaches promptly and effectively. Logging and log analysis are vital for security and compliance. Logging should be enabled for all relevant PaaS components and applications. Logs should be securely stored, and automated log analysis tools can help identify security issues or unusual behavior. Regularly reviewing logs can *aid in detecting and mitigating security threats. Security by design is a fundamental principle in PaaS security. Organizations should consider security throughout the entire application development lifecycle. This includes conducting security assessments and code reviews during the development phase, using secure coding practices, and performing security testing, such as penetration testing and code scanning. Security training and awareness programs should be implemented to educate development teams about best practices and potential security threats. Container security is crucial when deploying containerized applications on PaaS platforms. Containers should be configured securely, following best practices such as running containers with the least privilege and regularly updating container images with security patches. Organizations should also consider container security tools and vulnerability scanning solutions to ensure the security of containerized applications. Security orchestration and automation can enhance PaaS security. Automating security processes and responses can help organizations quickly detect and respond to security incidents. Security orchestration tools can help integrate security workflows, ensuring a coordinated and effective response. PaaS providers often offer security services and features that organizations can leverage to enhance their security posture. These may include firewall services, intrusion detection systems, and security information and event management (SIEM) solutions. Organizations should take advantage of these offerings to strengthen their PaaS security. Access control and* segregation of duties are critical in PaaS environments. Organizations should ensure that users and applications have the appropriate level of access, and access controls should be reviewed regularly. Segregation of duties helps prevent conflicts of interest and limits the potential for misuse of privileges. Organizations should also implement network security best practices. This includes using virtual private clouds (VPCs) or network security groups (NSGs) to control inbound and outbound traffic to PaaS resources. Network security policies should be enforced to protect against distributed denial-of-service (DDoS) attacks and other network-based threats. Regular security assessments and third-party security audits can provide an independent evaluation of an organization's PaaS security controls. These assessments help identify potential weaknesses and areas for improvement in the security posture. Security standards and best practices should be documented and communicated across the organization. This ensures that security policies and procedures are followed consistently. Security awareness training programs can help employees and teams understand their roles in maintaining PaaS security. In summary, PaaS security best practices are essential for organizations to protect their cloud-based applications and data. These practices encompass identity and access management, encryption, data privacy and compliance, security patch management, vulnerability scanning, continuous monitoring, incident response, logging, security by design, container security, security orchestration and automation, leveraging PaaS provider security features, *access control, network security, security assessments, documentation, and security awareness training. By implementing these best practices, organizations can establish a robust and effective security framework for their PaaS environments, mitigating risks and safeguarding their valuable assets. Meeting regulatory requirements in Platform as a Service (PaaS) environments is a critical concern for organizations in highly regulated industries, such as healthcare, finance, and government. Regulations, standards, and compliance frameworks are put in place to protect sensitive data, ensure data privacy, and establish security controls. One of the key regulatory frameworks that organizations often need to comply with is the General Data Protection Regulation (GDPR), which applies to the processing of personal data of European Union (EU) residents. Under GDPR, organizations must implement robust data protection measures, including encryption, access controls, and breach notification procedures, when handling personal data in PaaS environments. The Health Insurance Portability and Accountability Act (HIPAA) is another crucial regulation, particularly for healthcare organizations. HIPAA mandates strict safeguards for electronic protected health information (ePHI), including secure storage, access controls, audit trails, and breach reporting. Organizations using PaaS for healthcare applications must ensure that these safeguards are in place and regularly audited for compliance. The Payment Card Industry Data Security Standard (PCI DSS) is essential for businesses handling credit card data.*

When utilizing PaaS for e-commerce or payment processing, organizations must adhere to PCI DSS requirements, such as network segmentation, encryption, and regular security assessments. Government agencies often have specific compliance requirements, such as the Federal Risk and Authorization Management Program (FedRAMP) in the United States. FedRAMP outlines security controls and processes for cloud service providers (CSPs) hosting government data. PaaS providers seeking government clients must obtain FedRAMP certification to meet these requirements. Data sovereignty regulations are also crucial considerations. Certain countries and regions have strict rules about where data can be stored and processed. Organizations using PaaS need to ensure that data is hosted in compliance with these regulations, which may require choosing PaaS providers with data centers in specific geographic locations. Meeting regulatory requirements in PaaS starts with a thorough assessment of the relevant regulations and standards that apply to the organization's industry and data. Understanding the specific requirements and controls is essential before designing and deploying applications in the PaaS environment. Organizations should conduct a risk assessment to identify potential vulnerabilities and assess the impact of non-compliance. This assessment helps prioritize security measures and compliance efforts. PaaS providers often offer compliance documentation and resources to assist organizations in meeting regulatory requirements. Organizations should leverage these materials to understand how the PaaS provider addresses security and compliance concerns. Data classification and mapping are essential steps in meeting regulatory requirements. Organizations must classify data based on its sensitivity and importance. Mapping data flows and understanding how data moves within the PaaS environment is crucial for implementing proper access controls and encryption. Encryption is a fundamental security control for protecting data in PaaS environments. Organizations should implement encryption for data at rest and in transit, using strong encryption algorithms. Key management is a critical aspect of encryption, ensuring that encryption keys are properly protected and rotated as required by regulations. Access controls should be implemented to restrict access to data and resources in the PaaS environment. Role-based access control (RBAC) and least privilege principles help ensure that users and applications only have access to what is necessary for their roles. Audit trails and logging are necessary for compliance reporting and incident response. Organizations should enable logging for all relevant activities within the PaaS environment and retain logs for the required period. Regularly reviewing logs and conducting audits help identify security incidents and maintain compliance. Organizations should establish an incident response plan that outlines procedures for detecting, reporting, and mitigating security incidents. This plan should be tested and updated regularly to ensure effectiveness. Compliance reporting and documentation are crucial for demonstrating adherence to regulatory requirements. Organizations should maintain detailed records of security controls, assessments, and audits. Compliance reports may need to be submitted to regulatory authorities or third-party auditors. Training and awareness programs are essential for ensuring that employees and teams understand their roles in maintaining regulatory compliance. These programs help educate personnel about security policies, procedures, and best practices. Regular training and awareness efforts help create a culture of security within the organization. Third-party assessments and audits may be required to validate compliance with regulations. Organizations can engage independent auditors or assessors to evaluate their PaaS environment's compliance with specific regulations and standards. Regular assessments help identify areas for improvement and demonstrate a commitment to compliance. In summary, meeting regulatory requirements in PaaS environments involves understanding the relevant regulations, conducting risk assessments, classifying and mapping data, implementing encryption and access controls, maintaining audit trails, and establishing an incident response plan. Compliance reporting, documentation, training, and third-party assessments are also essential components of a comprehensive compliance strategy. By following these best practices and working closely with their PaaS providers, organizations can navigate the complex landscape of regulatory requirements and ensure that their PaaS environments meet the necessary compliance standards.

Chapter 10: Future Horizons: PaaS Innovations and Trends

Emerging technologies have a profound impact on Platform as a Service (PaaS) environments, shaping the future of application development and deployment. One of the most influential emerging technologies is artificial intelligence (AI). AI capabilities are increasingly integrated into PaaS platforms, allowing developers to incorporate machine learning and natural language processing into their applications. This empowers organizations to build more intelligent and responsive applications that can analyze data, make predictions, and interact with users in a more natural way. Edge computing is another technology that is transforming PaaS. With the proliferation of IoT devices and the need for low-latency processing, edge computing brings computational power closer to the data source. PaaS providers are offering edge PaaS solutions that enable developers to deploy and manage applications at the edge of the network, reducing latency and improving real-time processing. Serverless computing is gaining traction as a paradigm shift in PaaS. With serverless platforms, developers can focus on writing code without the need to manage servers or infrastructure. PaaS providers offer serverless environments where applications automatically scale and handle the underlying infrastructure, allowing for efficient resource utilization and cost savings. Blockchain technology is impacting PaaS by providing a secure and tamper-resistant way to record and verify transactions. PaaS offerings are incorporating blockchain capabilities, making it easier for organizations to build applications with transparency and trust. Containerization and container orchestration continue to evolve in the PaaS landscape. Containers, managed by technologies like Docker and Kubernetes, enable the packaging of applications and their dependencies in a consistent and portable format. PaaS providers are embracing containers, allowing developers to build, deploy, and scale containerized applications seamlessly. Quantum computing is an emerging technology with the potential to revolutionize PaaS. While quantum computing is in its infancy, PaaS providers are exploring how to integrate quantum capabilities into their platforms to address complex problems in areas like cryptography, optimization, and scientific research. 5G technology is poised to bring ultra-high-speed, low-latency connectivity to PaaS environments. This will enable applications that require real-time data processing, such as augmented reality, virtual reality, and autonomous vehicles, to flourish on PaaS platforms. Edge AI combines edge computing and artificial intelligence, enabling intelligent decision-making at the edge of the network. PaaS providers are exploring how to support edge AI applications, where data is processed locally on edge devices, reducing latency and dependence on cloud resources. IoT platforms are an integral part of PaaS, enabling the management and analysis of data from connected devices. As IoT adoption grows, PaaS providers are enhancing their IoT offerings to provide scalable, secure, and efficient solutions for IoT application development. Container-native development tools are emerging to simplify the development and deployment of containerized applications on PaaS platforms. These tools streamline the containerization process, making it easier for developers to package and distribute their applications. Low-code and no-code platforms are changing the landscape of PaaS by allowing users with limited coding experience to build applications using visual interfaces and pre-built components. These platforms democratize application development and reduce the barrier to entry for creating software. Open-source technologies continue to play a significant role in shaping PaaS environments. Many PaaS providers leverage open-source projects like Kubernetes, Prometheus, and Istio to enhance their offerings and provide more robust and flexible solutions. Quantum-safe cryptography is an emerging field focused on developing encryption algorithms that can withstand attacks from quantum computers. PaaS providers are exploring quantum-safe encryption to ensure data security in a post-quantum computing world. Graph databases are gaining popularity as organizations seek more efficient ways to analyze and visualize complex relationships in data. PaaS platforms are integrating graph database capabilities to support applications in areas such as social networking, fraud detection, and recommendation systems. Digital twins are virtual representations of physical objects or systems. PaaS environments are starting to incorporate digital twin technologies, enabling organizations to create and manage digital twins for various use cases, including predictive maintenance and simulations. Augmented reality (AR) and virtual reality (VR) are becoming more prevalent in PaaS as organizations explore immersive experiences and training applications. PaaS providers are developing AR and VR development tools and hosting environments to support these emerging technologies. Blockchain-based smart contracts are automating business processes and agreements in a trustless and secure manner. PaaS platforms are exploring how to facilitate the development and execution of smart contracts, opening up new possibilities for decentralized applications. Robotic Process Automation (RPA) is automating repetitive tasks and processes using software robots. PaaS providers are looking into RPA integration to help organizations streamline workflows and improve efficiency. Natural Language Processing (NLP) and chatbots are enhancing customer service and communication in PaaS applications. These technologies enable chatbots to understand and respond to user queries in a conversational manner. Multi-cloud and hybrid cloud strategies are becoming more prevalent as organizations seek to leverage the strengths of different cloud providers. PaaS offerings are evolving to support multi-cloud and hybrid cloud deployments, allowing applications to run seamlessly across various cloud environments. Quantum machine learning is a fusion of quantum computing and machine learning, promising faster and more efficient algorithms for data analysis and pattern recognition. PaaS providers are exploring how to enable quantum machine learning capabilities for data-driven applications. Digital ethics and responsible AI are gaining importance in PaaS environments. PaaS providers are emphasizing ethical considerations and responsible AI practices to ensure that AI-driven applications adhere to ethical guidelines and avoid bias and discrimination. In summary, emerging technologies are shaping the future of PaaS by introducing new capabilities, improving efficiency, and expanding the possibilities of application development and deployment. AI, edge computing, serverless computing, blockchain, containerization, quantum computing, 5G, edge AI, IoT platforms, container-native development tools, low-code/no-code platforms, open-source technologies, quantum-safe cryptography, graph databases, digital twins, AR/VR, blockchain-based smart contracts, RPA, NLP/chatbots, multi-cloud/hybrid cloud strategies, quantum machine learning, and digital ethics are all influencing the PaaS landscape. Organizations that embrace these technologies and adapt to the evolving PaaS ecosystem will be better positioned to innovate and thrive in the digital era. Predicting the future of Platform as a Service (PaaS) development is a challenging yet essential task in a rapidly evolving technology landscape. As we look ahead, several key trends and predictions emerge that are likely to shape the future of PaaS. First and foremost, the adoption of PaaS is expected to continue to grow across industries. Organizations are increasingly recognizing the benefits of PaaS, such as agility, scalability, and cost-

effectiveness, making it a fundamental component of their IT strategies. This growth is driven by the ongoing shift towards cloud-native development and the demand for faster application delivery. As PaaS platforms evolve, we can expect to see more emphasis on developer-centric features and capabilities. PaaS providers will invest in tools, services, and resources that empower developers to build, deploy, and manage applications more efficiently. This developer-centric approach will foster innovation and accelerate the development of new applications and services. One of the most significant trends in PaaS development is the continued integration of artificial intelligence (AI) and machine learning (ML) capabilities. PaaS platforms will increasingly offer AI and ML services that allow developers to incorporate predictive analytics, natural language processing, and computer vision into their applications. These AI-powered features will enable applications to become more intelligent, responsive, and capable of delivering personalized user experiences. Serverless computing is expected to gain even more prominence in the PaaS landscape. As organizations seek to reduce operational overhead and focus on code development, serverless platforms will become the go-to choice for many application workloads. Serverless architectures, combined with event-driven programming models, will enable developers to create highly scalable and cost-efficient applications. Edge computing will play a pivotal role in the future of PaaS development. The proliferation of IoT devices and the need for real-time processing will drive the adoption of edge PaaS solutions. Developers will leverage these platforms to deploy applications closer to the data source, reducing latency and enabling new use cases in areas such as autonomous vehicles and smart cities. Security will remain a top priority in PaaS development. With the increasing frequency and sophistication of cyberattacks, PaaS providers will invest heavily in enhancing security measures. We can expect to see advancements in encryption, threat detection, and identity and access management (IAM) to protect both applications and data. Multi-cloud and hybrid cloud strategies will become the norm in PaaS development. Organizations will leverage multiple cloud providers to diversify risk, enhance resilience, and access unique features. PaaS platforms will adapt to provide seamless support for multi-cloud and hybrid cloud deployments, simplifying management and orchestration across different environments. Containerization and container orchestration will continue to be foundational in PaaS development. Containers, powered by technologies like Docker and Kubernetes, provide a standardized and portable way to package and deploy applications. PaaS providers will expand their container offerings to streamline containerized application development and management. Quantum computing, while still in its infancy, will start to impact PaaS development. As quantum computing capabilities mature, PaaS providers will explore ways to integrate quantum computing resources and services into their platforms. This integration will unlock new possibilities for solving complex problems and optimizing applications. The democratization of technology will drive inclusivity in PaaS development. Low-code and no-code platforms will empower individuals with varying levels of technical expertise to participate in application development. This democratization will lead to a more diverse and creative developer ecosystem. Inclusivity also extends to digital ethics and responsible AI. As AI becomes more prevalent in PaaS applications, ethical considerations will become increasingly important. PaaS providers will focus on promoting responsible AI practices, addressing issues of bias, transparency, and fairness in AI-driven applications. PaaS development will continue to be influenced by open-source technologies. Open-source projects like Kubernetes, Prometheus, and Istio will play a significant role in shaping PaaS platforms and expanding their capabilities. PaaS providers will actively contribute to and collaborate with the open-source community. The convergence of DevOps and PaaS will accelerate the development and deployment of applications. DevOps practices, combined with PaaS automation, will enable continuous integration and continuous delivery (CI/CD) pipelines to become more streamlined and efficient. This convergence will reduce time-to-market and enhance application quality. Lastly, the future of PaaS development will be marked by a strong emphasis on sustainability. As environmental concerns grow, PaaS providers will invest in energy-efficient data centers and eco-friendly practices. Sustainable PaaS solutions will align with organizations' environmental goals and contribute to a greener future. In summary, the future of PaaS development is characterized by continued growth, developer-centric innovation, AI and ML integration, serverless computing, edge computing, enhanced security, multi-cloud and hybrid cloud strategies, containerization, quantum computing, democratization, digital ethics, open-source collaboration, DevOps convergence, and sustainability. These trends and predictions collectively shape the path forward for PaaS, promising a future of increased agility, innovation, and responsible technology usage.

BOOK 3
Platform as a Service Unleashed
A Comprehensive Guide to Google Cloud, Microsoft
Azure, and IBM Cloud

ROB BOTWRIGHT

Chapter 1: Introduction to Platform as a Service (PaaS)

Platform as a Service, often abbreviated as PaaS, is a cloud computing service model that provides a comprehensive environment for developing, deploying, and managing applications over the internet. At its core, PaaS offers a platform with tools, services, and infrastructure that simplifies the software development lifecycle. This includes everything from coding and testing to deploying and maintaining applications. PaaS sits in the middle of the cloud service models, with Infrastructure as a Service (IaaS) providing the foundational compute, storage, and networking resources, and Software as a Service (SaaS) delivering fully functional applications to end-users. The primary aim of PaaS is to empower developers by abstracting away the complexities of infrastructure management. In a PaaS environment, developers can focus on writing code and building features rather than dealing with the underlying hardware or software stack. This abstraction allows for faster application development and deployment cycles. A key characteristic of PaaS is its scalability. PaaS platforms are designed to automatically scale resources up or down based on demand. This elasticity ensures that applications can handle fluctuations in traffic and workload without manual intervention. PaaS providers typically offer a range of development tools and services. These tools often include integrated development environments (IDEs), programming languages, frameworks, databases, and middleware. Developers can access these resources on the cloud platform, making it convenient to build and test applications. PaaS also supports collaboration among development teams. Multiple developers can work on the same project simultaneously, leveraging version control systems and collaboration tools integrated into the platform. This fosters teamwork and accelerates the development process. Another critical aspect of PaaS is its ability to streamline application deployment. PaaS platforms provide tools and services for packaging and deploying applications, making it easier to move from development to production. These platforms often support continuous integration and continuous delivery (CI/CD) pipelines, allowing for automated testing and deployment workflows. PaaS offers a range of deployment options. Developers can choose to deploy applications on public cloud platforms, private clouds, or hybrid environments, depending on their specific needs and requirements. PaaS also abstracts away many administrative tasks. While developers are responsible for writing application code, PaaS providers manage the underlying infrastructure, including servers, storage, and networking. This reduces the operational burden on development teams. Security is a vital consideration in PaaS. PaaS providers implement robust security measures to protect applications and data. These measures include encryption, access controls, identity and access management (IAM), and security monitoring. PaaS also enables organizations to implement compliance requirements more easily. Many PaaS providers offer compliance certifications, simplifying the process of adhering to industry-specific regulations. The scope of PaaS is continually expanding as technology evolves. PaaS was initially designed for web application development, but its scope has broadened to include a wide range of use cases. Today, PaaS supports the development of mobile applications, microservices, IoT applications, and more. It also extends beyond traditional coding to include low-code and no-code development platforms. Low-code platforms enable users with limited coding experience to build applications using visual interfaces and pre-built components. No-code platforms take this a step further, allowing business users to create applications without writing any code. This democratization of application development opens up new possibilities for organizations. PaaS platforms are also embracing containerization and container orchestration. Containers, powered by technologies like Docker, provide a consistent and portable way to package and deploy applications and their dependencies. Kubernetes, a popular container orchestration platform, is often integrated into PaaS environments to simplify container management. Quantum computing is an emerging field that is starting to intersect with PaaS. While quantum computing is in its infancy, PaaS providers are exploring how to support quantum applications and services. This could lead to new opportunities for solving complex problems and optimizing applications. PaaS is also evolving to address the challenges of edge computing. Edge PaaS solutions are designed to deploy and manage *applications at the edge of the network, closer to the data source. This reduces latency and enables real-time processing for applications like IoT and autonomous vehicles. As the technology landscape continues to evolve, the scope of PaaS will likely expand further. PaaS providers will adapt to incorporate emerging technologies, tools, and services that empower developers and organizations to innovate and stay competitive. In summary, Platform as a Service (PaaS) is a cloud computing service model that provides a platform with tools, services, and infrastructure for developing, deploying, and managing applications. PaaS abstracts away the complexities of infrastructure management, allowing developers to focus on coding and building features. It offers scalability, a range of development tools, collaboration capabilities, streamlined deployment, and security. The scope of PaaS has expanded to include mobile applications, microservices, IoT, low-code/no-code development, containerization, quantum computing, and edge computing. As technology continues to evolve, PaaS will adapt to support emerging trends and empower organizations to innovate in the digital age. The evolution of cloud service models has been a transformative journey in the world of technology and computing. It has reshaped the way organizations access and manage their IT resources. The journey began with the advent of cloud computing itself, a paradigm shift that moved computing resources from on-premises data centers to remote, off-site locations. At its core, cloud computing aimed to provide a scalable and cost-effective alternative to traditional IT infrastructure. The earliest cloud service models were Infrastructure as a Service (IaaS) and Platform as a Service (PaaS). IaaS offered virtualized computing resources, including virtual machines, storage, and networking, allowing users to provision and manage infrastructure components in the cloud. This was a significant departure from the traditional model of purchasing and maintaining physical servers. PaaS, on the other hand, provided a higher level of abstraction by offering a platform with development tools, services, and middleware to facilitate application development and deployment. Developers could build and run applications without the need to manage underlying infrastructure. These early cloud service models laid the foundation for the cloud computing revolution. They introduced concepts like resource pooling, self-service provisioning, and pay-as-you-go pricing, which became fundamental to cloud computing. As cloud adoption grew, a new service model emerged - Software as a Service (SaaS). SaaS represented a shift in focus from infrastructure and platforms to fully functional software applications delivered over the internet. Users could access software applications through web browsers, eliminating the need for local installations and updates. This model proved particularly attractive for businesses seeking cost-effective and user-friendly solutions, leading to the proliferation of cloud-based email, collaboration, and productivity tools. The rise of SaaS also brought about the concept of multi-tenancy, where a single instance of an application serves multiple* customers, each with their own isolated data and configurations. SaaS providers managed application maintenance, updates, and scalability, relieving users of these responsibilities. With the success of SaaS, the cloud landscape continued to evolve. A new service model, Function as a Service (FaaS), emerged, popularly known as serverless computing. Serverless computing took abstraction to the extreme by abstracting away servers altogether. Developers could write code in the form of functions or microservices and deploy them in a serverless environment. The underlying infrastructure, scaling, and resource management were entirely handled by the cloud provider. This model introduced the concept of "pay only for what you use," as users were billed based on the actual execution of functions rather than reserving and paying for server capacity. Serverless computing enabled rapid development and deployment of event-driven, highly scalable applications. As cloud technology advanced, new considerations emerged, such as data analytics, artificial intelligence (AI), and machine learning (ML). These requirements gave rise to specialized cloud service models like Data Analytics as a Service, AI as a Service, and ML as a Service. These models offered pre-configured environments and tools for data processing, analysis, and model training. Developers and data scientists could leverage these services to gain insights, build predictive models, and enhance their applications without needing in-depth expertise in data science or AI. The concept of edge computing also became increasingly important as the Internet of Things (IoT) gained momentum. Edge computing brought computing resources closer to data sources, reducing latency and enabling real-time processing for applications like autonomous vehicles, industrial automation, and smart cities. Edge computing service models extended cloud computing to the edge of the network, facilitating the deployment and management of applications in edge environments. Hybrid cloud solutions emerged as organizations sought to combine the benefits of both on-premises and cloud infrastructure. Hybrid cloud service models allowed seamless integration between private, on-premises data centers and public cloud resources. This flexibility enabled organizations to leverage the cloud's scalability while maintaining control and security over their IT infrastructure. With the growth of cloud-native technologies like containers and microservices, Container as a Service (CaaS) and Microservices as a Service (MaaS) models gained traction. CaaS provided managed container orchestration platforms, such as Kubernetes, while MaaS offered tools and services to develop, deploy, and manage microservices-based applications. These service models supported modern application architectures designed for agility, scalability, and resilience. Quantum computing, an emerging field, is expected to impact cloud service models in the future. Quantum as a Service (QaaS) could provide access to quantum computing resources, allowing researchers and organizations to explore quantum algorithms and solve complex problems. The evolution of cloud service models continues as technology continues to advance. Future *developments may include new service models tailored to emerging technologies like quantum computing, digital twins, and decentralized applications (DApps). These service models will continue to shape the way organizations leverage cloud computing to innovate, compete, and meet their IT needs. In summary, the evolution of cloud service models has been a transformative journey that began with IaaS and PaaS, expanded to include SaaS, serverless computing, specialized models for data analytics and AI, edge computing, hybrid cloud, and cloud-native technologies. This evolution reflects the ever-changing landscape of technology and the growing demands of organizations for flexibility, scalability, and innovation in the cloud.*

Chapter 2: PaaS Fundamentals and Advantages

To understand Platform as a Service (PaaS) fully, it's essential to grasp several key concepts that underpin this cloud computing model. At its core, PaaS is a cloud service that provides a comprehensive platform for application development, deployment, and management. One fundamental concept in PaaS is the abstraction of infrastructure. PaaS abstracts away the complexities of hardware, servers, and networking, allowing developers to focus solely on building and deploying applications. This abstraction simplifies the development process and reduces the operational burden on development teams. Another crucial concept is the developer-centric approach. PaaS platforms prioritize the needs of developers by offering a wide range of tools, services, and resources. These include integrated development environments (IDEs), programming languages, libraries, databases, and middleware. Developers can access and leverage these resources directly from the PaaS platform, streamlining the development process. PaaS platforms also support collaboration among development teams. Multiple developers can work on the same project simultaneously, using version control systems and collaboration tools integrated into the platform. This fosters teamwork, accelerates development, and enables organizations to efficiently build and maintain their applications. Scalability is a key concept in PaaS.

PaaS platforms are designed to be scalable, meaning they can automatically allocate and deallocate resources based on application demand. This elasticity ensures that applications can handle fluctuations in traffic without manual intervention. Security is a fundamental concern in PaaS. PaaS providers implement robust security measures to protect both applications and data. These measures include encryption, access controls, identity and access management (IAM), and security monitoring. PaaS platforms are also designed to facilitate compliance with industry-specific regulations, making it easier for organizations to meet their compliance requirements. Data storage and management are central to PaaS. PaaS platforms typically offer various data storage solutions, including relational databases, NoSQL databases, and data warehouses. These storage options cater to different application needs, ensuring that data is stored, accessed, and managed efficiently. Deployment is a core concept in PaaS. PaaS platforms provide tools and services for packaging and deploying applications. Developers can use these platforms to move applications from development to production environments with ease. Continuous integration and continuous delivery (CI/CD) pipelines are often supported, enabling automated testing and deployment workflows. One of the distinguishing features of PaaS is its billing model. PaaS operates on a pay-as-you-go or subscription-based pricing model. Users are billed based on their usage of platform resources, making it cost-effective and scalable. This model contrasts with traditional IT infrastructure, where organizations must purchase and maintain hardware and software licenses upfront. PaaS encourages a "pay only for what you use" philosophy, aligning costs with actual resource consumption. The concept of multi-cloud and hybrid cloud is also relevant to PaaS. Multi-cloud refers to the practice of using multiple cloud providers to diversify risk, enhance resilience, and access unique features. Hybrid cloud combines on-premises infrastructure with cloud resources, allowing organizations to leverage the benefits of both. PaaS platforms adapt to support multi-cloud and hybrid cloud deployments, simplifying management and orchestration across different environments. Containerization and container orchestration are vital concepts in modern PaaS. Containers, powered by technologies like Docker, provide a standardized and portable way to package and deploy applications and their dependencies. Kubernetes, a popular container orchestration platform, is often integrated into PaaS environments to simplify container management. Serverless computing, often referred to as Function as a Service (FaaS), is a disruptive concept in PaaS. Serverless computing abstracts away servers entirely, allowing developers to write code in the form of functions or microservices. The underlying infrastructure, scaling, and resource management are entirely handled by the cloud provider. Developers are billed based on the actual execution of functions, making it highly cost-efficient and suitable for event-driven applications. Edge computing extends cloud computing to the edge of the network. Edge PaaS *solutions enable the deployment and management of applications closer to data sources, reducing latency and enabling real-time processing. This concept is particularly relevant for applications in IoT, autonomous vehicles, and smart cities. Low-code and no-code development are democratizing concepts in PaaS. Low-code platforms enable users with limited coding experience to build applications using visual interfaces and pre-built components. No-code platforms go further by allowing business users to create applications without writing any code. These concepts democratize application development, making it accessible to a broader audience. Open-source technologies play a significant role in PaaS. Many PaaS providers leverage open-source projects like Kubernetes, Prometheus, and Istio to enhance their offerings and provide more robust and flexible solutions. The concept of digital ethics and responsible AI is gaining importance in PaaS. As AI becomes more prevalent in PaaS applications, ethical considerations become increasingly important. PaaS providers are emphasizing responsible AI practices to ensure that AI-driven applications adhere to ethical guidelines, avoid bias, and maintain transparency. In summary, key concepts in PaaS encompass infrastructure abstraction, developer-centricity, collaboration, scalability, security, compliance, data management, deployment, billing models, multi-cloud and hybrid cloud, containerization, serverless computing, edge computing, low-code/no-code development, open source, and digital ethics. These concepts collectively define the foundation and* principles of Platform as a Service, making it a powerful and flexible cloud computing model for modern application development and deployment. The adoption of Platform as a Service (PaaS) offers organizations numerous advantages and benefits that can positively impact their operations and development efforts. One of the primary advantages of PaaS is the accelerated development cycle it enables. By abstracting infrastructure management, developers can focus their efforts on coding and building features, significantly reducing time-to-market for applications. This increased speed of development allows organizations to respond more quickly to changing market demands and gain a competitive edge. PaaS also fosters innovation by providing developers with a wide range of development tools and services. These tools often include integrated development environments (IDEs), programming languages, libraries, and pre-built components, empowering developers to explore creative solutions and build cutting-edge applications. In addition to fostering innovation, PaaS supports collaboration among development teams. Multiple developers can work on the same project simultaneously, using version control systems and collaboration tools integrated into the platform. This collaboration enhances teamwork, accelerates development, and ensures efficient project management. Scalability is another significant benefit of PaaS adoption. PaaS platforms are designed to automatically scale resources up or down based on application demand. This elasticity ensures that applications can handle fluctuations in traffic without manual intervention, ensuring a seamless user experience. PaaS also simplifies resource management, as the cloud provider handles the underlying infrastructure, including servers, storage, and networking. This reduces the operational burden on development teams, allowing them to focus on coding and application development. PaaS platforms offer robust security measures to protect both applications and data. Security features often include encryption, access controls, identity and access management (IAM), and security monitoring. PaaS providers also facilitate compliance with industry-specific regulations, making it easier for organizations to meet their compliance requirements. Data storage and management are central to many applications, and PaaS platforms offer a variety of data storage solutions. These solutions include relational databases, NoSQL databases, and data warehouses, catering to different application needs and ensuring efficient data handling. PaaS platforms provide tools and services for packaging and deploying applications, simplifying the deployment process. Continuous integration and continuous delivery (CI/CD) pipelines are often supported, allowing for automated testing and deployment workflows. The billing model of PaaS aligns with a "pay only for what you use" philosophy, making it cost-effective and scalable. Users are billed based on their actual resource consumption, eliminating the need to purchase and maintain hardware or software licenses upfront. PaaS encourages cost efficiency by optimizing resource allocation and usage. The multi-cloud and hybrid cloud capabilities of

PaaS offer organizations flexibility in choosing their cloud deployment models. Multi-cloud strategies allow organizations to diversify risk, enhance resilience, and access unique cloud features. Hybrid cloud solutions combine on-premises infrastructure with cloud resources, providing the benefits of both worlds. PaaS platforms adapt to support multi-cloud and hybrid cloud deployments, simplifying management and orchestration across different environments. Containerization and container orchestration are essential concepts in modern PaaS, providing a standardized and portable way to package and deploy applications. Containers, powered by technologies like Docker, streamline the development and deployment process, enhancing agility and scalability. Serverless computing, often referred to as Function as a Service (FaaS), is a disruptive concept in PaaS that abstracts away servers entirely. Developers can write code in the form of functions or microservices, and the cloud provider handles the underlying infrastructure, scaling, and resource management. This model ensures high cost-efficiency, as users are billed based on the actual execution of functions. Edge computing extends PaaS to the edge of the network, enabling real-time processing for applications like IoT, autonomous vehicles, and smart cities. Edge PaaS solutions reduce latency and improve responsiveness by deploying applications closer to data sources. Low-code and no-code development platforms democratize application development, allowing users with limited coding experience to build applications using visual interfaces and pre-built *components. These platforms empower a broader audience to participate in application development, reducing the time and expertise required to create software. Open-source technologies play a significant role in PaaS, with many providers leveraging open-source projects to enhance their offerings. Open-source projects like Kubernetes, Prometheus, and Istio contribute to the robustness and flexibility of PaaS platforms. Digital ethics and responsible AI practices are emphasized in PaaS environments, ensuring that AI-driven applications adhere to ethical guidelines, avoid bias, and maintain transparency. In summary, the adoption of PaaS brings numerous advantages and benefits to organizations, including accelerated development cycles, innovation, collaboration, scalability, simplified resource management, robust security, compliance support, efficient data handling, streamlined deployment, cost-effectiveness, multi-cloud and hybrid cloud capabilities, containerization, serverless computing, edge computing, low-code/no-code development, open-source integration, and a focus on digital ethics and responsible AI. These advantages collectively make PaaS a powerful and flexible cloud computing model that empowers organizations to thrive in the digital era.*

Chapter 3: Exploring Google Cloud Platform's PaaS Offerings

Google Cloud Platform (GCP) offers a comprehensive suite of Platform as a Service (PaaS) services that empower organizations to build, deploy, and manage applications with ease. GCP's PaaS offerings encompass a wide range of tools and services designed to streamline the application development and deployment process. At the heart of GCP's PaaS services is Google App Engine, a fully managed platform that allows developers to build and deploy applications without worrying about infrastructure management. Google App Engine supports multiple programming languages, including Python, Java, PHP, and Node.js, making it accessible to a diverse developer community. One of the key benefits of Google App Engine is its automatic scaling capabilities, which enable applications to handle varying levels of traffic and load without manual intervention. Developers can focus on writing code while Google App Engine takes care of resource allocation and scaling. GCP's PaaS offerings also include Google Cloud Functions, a serverless computing platform that allows developers to run single-purpose functions in response to events. This event-driven architecture is highly efficient and cost-effective, as users only pay for the actual execution of functions. Google Cloud Functions is ideal for building lightweight and responsive applications that can scale automatically based on demand. Another essential component of GCP's PaaS services is Google Kubernetes Engine (GKE), a managed Kubernetes service. Kubernetes is a container orchestration platform that simplifies the deployment, scaling, and management of containerized applications. GKE abstracts away the complexities of managing Kubernetes clusters, allowing developers to focus on building containerized applications. GKE provides features such as automated scaling, load balancing, and rolling updates, making it an excellent choice for containerized workloads. GCP's PaaS offerings extend to databases and data management, with services like Google Cloud SQL and Google Cloud Firestore. Google Cloud SQL is a fully managed relational database service that supports MySQL, PostgreSQL, and SQL Server. It offers automated backups, high availability, and scalability, allowing developers to focus on database design and application development. Google Cloud Firestore is a NoSQL document database that provides real-time synchronization and offline data access for web and mobile applications. Firestore's serverless and globally distributed architecture makes it suitable for building responsive and scalable applications. For data analytics and machine learning, GCP offers services like Google BigQuery and Google Cloud AI Platform. Google BigQuery is a fully managed, serverless data warehouse that allows organizations to analyze large datasets with blazing speed and scalability. It supports standard SQL and integrates seamlessly with other GCP services. Google Cloud AI Platform provides a robust environment for developing, training, and deploying machine learning models at scale. It includes tools and services for data preprocessing, model training, and model deployment, making it accessible to data scientists and developers alike. Google Cloud Pub/Sub is a messaging service that facilitates event-driven communication between applications and services. It provides reliable and scalable messaging capabilities, enabling real-time data streaming and event processing. Pub/Sub is suitable for building applications that require event-driven architectures and data integration. In addition to these core services, GCP offers specialized PaaS services for various use cases. For example, Google Cloud Run allows developers to deploy containerized applications as serverless functions, combining the benefits of containers and serverless computing. Google Cloud Composer is a managed workflow orchestration service that simplifies the development and execution of data pipelines and workflows. It integrates with popular open-source tools like Apache Airflow. Google Cloud Dataflow is a fully managed stream and batch data processing service that simplifies data analytics and ETL (Extract, Transform, Load) tasks. These specialized services cater to specific application needs and workflows, providing developers with a rich ecosystem of tools to choose from. GCP's PaaS services are complemented by a robust set of developer tools and integrations. Google Cloud Build offers continuous integration and continuous delivery (CI/CD) capabilities, allowing developers to automate the building, testing, and deployment of applications. It integrates seamlessly with other GCP services and supports popular source *code repositories. Google Cloud Source Repositories provide version control and collaboration features for developers working on GCP projects. They support Git, making it easy to manage code and collaborate with team members. Google Cloud Debugger allows developers to inspect and debug applications in production without impacting end-users. It provides real-time debugging capabilities, making it easier to identify and resolve issues. GCP's PaaS services are known for their strong emphasis on security and compliance. Google Cloud Identity and Access Management (IAM) enables fine-grained access control, ensuring that only authorized users and services can access resources. GCP also offers robust encryption at rest and in transit, as well as integrated security and threat detection tools. For organizations with specific compliance requirements, GCP provides a wide range of certifications, including SOC 2, ISO 27001, HIPAA, and PCI DSS, making it suitable for industries such as healthcare, finance, and government. In summary, GCP's PaaS services offer a comprehensive and flexible platform for application development and deployment. With a wide range of tools and services, developers can build, scale, and manage applications efficiently. GCP's strong emphasis on security, compliance, and integration makes it a compelling choice for organizations seeking to leverage the power of the cloud for their applications and data workloads. Google Cloud Platform (GCP) offers a range of Platform as a Service (PaaS) solutions that cater to diverse use cases and industries. These PaaS solutions provide* organizations with the tools and capabilities needed to address specific business needs and challenges. One common use case for GCP's PaaS solutions is web application development. Organizations can leverage services like Google App Engine, which provides a fully managed platform for building and deploying web applications. App Engine supports multiple programming languages, making it accessible to a broad developer community. Developers can focus on coding and application logic, while GCP handles the underlying infrastructure, including scaling and resource allocation. This simplifies the development process and accelerates time-to-market for web applications. Another use case is the development of mobile applications. Google Cloud Firestore, a NoSQL document database, is well-suited for mobile app development. Firestore offers real-time synchronization and offline data access, critical features for responsive mobile apps. Developers can build mobile applications that provide a seamless user experience, even in scenarios with limited or unreliable network connectivity. GCP's PaaS solutions also find application in the field of data analytics. Google BigQuery, a serverless data warehouse, is ideal for organizations seeking to analyze large datasets and gain insights. BigQuery supports standard SQL and integrates seamlessly with other GCP services, making it a powerful tool for data analysts and data scientists. Organizations can perform complex data queries and analytics tasks without the need for infrastructure management. Machine learning is another area where GCP's PaaS solutions excel. Google Cloud AI Platform provides a robust environment for developing, training, and deploying machine learning models. Data scientists and developers can leverage AI Platform's tools and services for data preprocessing, model training, and model deployment. This use case is particularly relevant for organizations looking to harness the power of artificial intelligence to improve decision-making and automate tasks. GCP's PaaS solutions also play a significant role in supporting e-commerce applications. Google Kubernetes Engine (GKE), a managed Kubernetes service, provides a scalable and reliable platform for hosting e-commerce websites and applications. Retailers can ensure high availability, efficient scaling, and seamless customer experiences by running their e-commerce platforms on GKE. For organizations looking to implement event-driven architectures and real-time data processing, Google Cloud Pub/Sub is a valuable PaaS solution. It facilitates the integration of applications and services through reliable and scalable messaging capabilities. Pub/Sub is suitable for use cases such as IoT (Internet of Things), financial transactions, and real-time analytics, where timely event processing is essential. Google Cloud Functions, a serverless computing platform, is ideal for microservices-based architectures. Organizations can decompose their applications into smaller, independent functions that are triggered in response to events. This modular approach simplifies application development, deployment, and maintenance. For organizations that require workflow orchestration and data pipeline management, Google Cloud Composer is a PaaS solution *that provides a managed environment for building and executing workflows. Using Composer, organizations can automate and streamline complex business processes, such as data extraction, transformation, and loading (ETL), and gain operational efficiency. GCP's PaaS solutions extend to the realm of content management. Google Cloud Storage provides scalable and durable object storage, making it suitable for hosting and serving media files, documents, and user-generated content. Content management systems and media distribution platforms can benefit from GCP's reliable storage infrastructure. Serverless computing, as offered by Google Cloud Functions, is valuable for processing user-generated content and media files in response to user interactions. For organizations looking to develop IoT applications, GCP's PaaS solutions provide the necessary tools and services. Google Cloud IoT Core offers a fully managed platform for connecting, managing, and ingesting data from IoT devices. This enables organizations to build scalable and secure IoT solutions, whether for industrial automation, smart cities, or consumer devices. Edge computing, facilitated by Google Cloud IoT Edge and Google Kubernetes Engine (GKE) on edge devices, extends cloud capabilities to the edge of the network. This is particularly relevant for applications that require low-latency processing, such as autonomous vehicles and industrial control systems. In the realm of gaming, GCP's PaaS solutions offer scalability and reliability. Google Cloud Firestore can serve as a backend database for multiplayer games, providing real-time synchronization of game state across players. Additionally, Google Kubernetes Engine (GKE) can handle the scaling and orchestration of game servers to ensure a smooth gaming experience, even during peak usage. For organizations seeking to implement real-time analytics and monitoring, Google Cloud Dataflow provides a fully managed stream and batch data processing service. Dataflow allows organizations to ingest, process, and analyze data in real-time, enabling them to make informed decisions and gain insights as events unfold. This use case is valuable in industries such as finance, healthcare, and logistics. Collaborative applications, such as project management tools and communication platforms, can benefit from the scalability and real-time capabilities of Google Cloud Firestore. Firestore's support for real-time synchronization enables multiple users to collaborate seamlessly on shared documents and projects. This use case extends to various industries where collaboration and document sharing are essential. In summary, GCP's PaaS solutions cater to a wide range of use cases across industries, including web application development, mobile app development, data analytics, machine learning, e-commerce, event-driven architectures, content management, IoT, edge computing, gaming, real-time analytics, and collaborative applications. These PaaS solutions empower organizations to leverage the cloud's flexibility, scalability, and managed services to address their specific business needs and challenges, ultimately driving innovation and efficiency.*

Chapter 4: Mastering PaaS in Microsoft Azure

Azure, Microsoft's cloud computing platform, offers a robust and extensive set of Platform as a Service (PaaS) capabilities that empower organizations to build, deploy, and manage applications efficiently and at scale. These PaaS offerings cover a wide spectrum of services, from application hosting and development to data storage and analytics. Azure's PaaS capabilities are designed to streamline the application development process and accelerate time-to-market for businesses across various industries. One of the core PaaS offerings in Azure is Azure App Service, a fully managed platform that simplifies the deployment and scaling of web applications, APIs, and mobile backends. App Service supports multiple programming languages, including .NET, Java, Node.js, Python, and PHP, making it accessible to a diverse developer community. Developers can focus on writing code while Azure takes care of the underlying infrastructure, including server provisioning, load balancing, and automatic scaling. This allows organizations to quickly build, deploy, and update applications without the operational overhead. Azure Functions, another key PaaS service, enables serverless computing, allowing developers to write event-driven functions that execute in response to triggers or events. Functions abstract away server management, enabling users to execute code snippets without worrying about provisioning or managing servers. This serverless approach simplifies application development, particularly for tasks like data processing, image analysis, and automation. Azure Kubernetes Service (AKS) provides managed Kubernetes orchestration, catering to organizations embracing containerized applications and microservices. AKS abstracts the complexity of managing Kubernetes clusters, making it easier for developers to deploy, scale, and manage containerized workloads. Azure Container Instances (ACI) complements AKS by providing serverless, container-based computing for scenarios that require rapid scaling and fine-grained control over individual containers. For organizations looking to build and deploy AI-powered applications, Azure offers Azure Machine Learning, a PaaS service designed for machine learning model development and deployment. Data scientists and developers can leverage Azure Machine Learning to build, train, and deploy machine learning models at scale, using a wide range of tools and frameworks. Azure Stream Analytics is another PaaS service tailored for real-time data processing and analytics. It allows organizations to ingest, process, and analyze streaming data from various sources, enabling real-time insights and decision-making. Stream Analytics is well-suited for use cases such as IoT (Internet of Things) data analysis, fraud detection, and monitoring. Azure provides a suite of PaaS services for data storage and management, catering to different needs and scenarios. Azure SQL Database offers a fully managed, relational database service that supports multiple database engines, including SQL Server and PostgreSQL.

It provides high availability, scalability, and built-in security features, making it an excellent choice for applications requiring structured data storage. Azure Cosmos DB is a globally distributed, multi-model database service designed for mission-critical applications. It offers high availability, low latency, and seamless scalability, making it suitable for globally distributed and highly responsive applications. For NoSQL data storage needs, Azure offers services like Azure Table Storage and Azure Blob Storage, which provide scalable and cost-effective storage options for unstructured and semi-structured data. Azure Data Lake Storage extends Azure's data storage capabilities, offering a secure and scalable data lake for big data analytics and data warehousing. Azure PaaS services are tightly integrated with Azure DevOps, providing organizations with a comprehensive set of tools for application lifecycle management. Azure DevOps encompasses services like Azure DevTest Labs for development and testing environments, Azure DevOps Boards for project tracking and work item management, Azure DevOps Repos for version control and code collaboration, and Azure DevOps Pipelines for continuous integration and continuous delivery (CI/CD). These services enable organizations to implement efficient development workflows, from coding to testing to deployment, in a seamless and automated manner. Azure Logic Apps is a PaaS service designed for building and orchestrating workflows and integrations. It provides a visual designer for creating workflows that connect various services, applications, and data sources, simplifying complex business processes. Logic Apps are used to automate tasks, streamline approvals, and integrate with third-party services, allowing organizations to improve operational efficiency. Azure Functions can also be integrated into Logic Apps, enabling serverless components within workflows. For organizations with IoT initiatives, Azure IoT Hub offers a managed service for connecting, monitoring, and managing IoT devices at scale. It provides robust device-to-cloud and cloud-to-device communication capabilities, as well as device management and security features. Azure IoT Hub is essential for organizations deploying IoT solutions, whether in industrial automation, smart cities, or connected devices. Azure offers PaaS services that cater to the needs of organizations in highly regulated industries. Azure Government and Azure Government Secret are specialized cloud environments designed to meet the stringent compliance and security requirements of government agencies and organizations dealing with classified information. These environments offer a subset of Azure PaaS services, ensuring that government and regulated industry customers can leverage the cloud while adhering to specific regulations and security standards. Azure's PaaS capabilities extend to application insights and monitoring with Azure Application Insights. This service provides real-time performance and error tracking for web applications and services. Developers and operations teams can gain visibility into application performance, diagnose issues, and improve the user experience. Azure Monitor complements Application Insights by providing a comprehensive monitoring solution for Azure resources. It offers insights into resource-level metrics, logs, and diagnostics, enabling organizations to optimize the performance and health of their cloud workloads. In the realm of serverless computing, Azure Functions offers advanced capabilities, such as Durable Functions, which allow developers to build stateful serverless workflows and orchestrations. Durable Functions enable scenarios like long-running processes, human interaction workflows, and complex event-driven architectures. Azure Logic Apps can also be integrated with Azure Functions to create serverless workflows with built-in resilience and state management. For organizations seeking to develop and deploy AI models efficiently, Azure Machine Learning Service provides a robust platform. It supports a variety of machine learning frameworks and languages, including Python and R, and offers tools for data preparation, model training, and deployment. Developers can leverage Azure Machine Learning Service to build predictive and analytical models that enhance their applications. Azure Cognitive Services further extend AI capabilities by providing pre-built AI models for tasks such as image recognition, speech recognition, language understanding, and more. These services enable organizations to infuse AI capabilities into their applications without the need for extensive AI expertise. In summary, Azure's PaaS capabilities cover a wide range of services and use cases, from application hosting and development to data storage and analytics to AI and machine learning.

These services empower organizations to build, deploy, and manage applications efficiently, whether they are web and mobile applications, containerized microservices, data-intensive analytics, or IoT solutions. Azure's strong integration with developer tools, security features, and compliance offerings makes it a compelling choice for organizations seeking to leverage the cloud for their digital transformation efforts, regardless of their industry or specific business requirements.

Chapter 5: Harnessing the Power of IBM Cloud PaaS Solutions

In the real world, organizations across various industries have harnessed the power of Azure's Platform as a Service (PaaS) offerings to address specific challenges and drive innovation. Let's explore some real-world scenarios where Azure PaaS solutions have made a significant impact. Consider a global e-commerce company that faces the challenge of handling massive spikes in website traffic during holiday sales events. By leveraging Azure App Service, the company can seamlessly scale its web applications to accommodate the increased load. Azure's automatic scaling capabilities ensure that the website remains responsive, preventing downtime and revenue loss. In the healthcare sector, a medical research institution is working on genomic analysis, which requires massive computational power. Azure Batch, a PaaS service, allows researchers to submit large-scale computing jobs, distributing them across a pool of virtual machines. This dramatically accelerates the analysis process, enabling researchers to make faster progress in their quest for breakthroughs in genomics. A retail chain with a vast network of physical stores seeks to enhance the in-store shopping experience by leveraging IoT technology. Azure IoT Hub enables the chain to connect and manage thousands of IoT devices in real-time. These devices include smart shelves that monitor inventory levels, *beacons that send personalized offers to shoppers' smartphones, and security cameras for in-store monitoring. The data collected from these devices is processed and analyzed using Azure Stream Analytics, providing insights into customer behavior and inventory management. In the financial industry, a global bank needs to comply with stringent regulatory requirements for data retention and security. Azure's PaaS offerings, including Azure SQL Database and Azure Key Vault, play a critical role. The bank securely stores sensitive customer data in Azure SQL Database, which provides built-in encryption, auditing, and compliance capabilities. Azure Key Vault ensures the safe management of cryptographic keys and secrets, further enhancing data protection. For organizations in the manufacturing sector, predictive maintenance is a key priority to reduce downtime and increase operational efficiency. Azure Machine Learning helps them build predictive maintenance models using historical data from sensors and equipment. These models predict when machinery is likely to fail, allowing for timely maintenance and preventing costly unplanned downtime. In the education sector, a university wants to provide a modern learning experience for students by offering online courses and interactive content. Azure Media Services allows the university to efficiently encode, store, and stream video content to students worldwide. Additionally, Azure Content Delivery Network (CDN) ensures that students can access course materials with low latency, regardless of their location. A transportation and logistics company faces the* challenge of optimizing its supply chain and delivery routes to reduce costs and improve delivery times. Azure's PaaS solutions, such as Azure Databricks and Azure Synapse Analytics, help the company analyze vast amounts of data. They gain insights into factors like traffic patterns, weather conditions, and delivery demand, enabling more efficient route planning and resource allocation. A startup in the gaming industry wants to launch a new mobile game that requires real-time multiplayer capabilities. Azure Cosmos DB, a globally distributed NoSQL database service, ensures low-latency, high-performance data access for players worldwide. Azure Functions are used to handle real-time game events, ensuring a seamless and responsive gaming experience. A non-profit organization focuses on disaster response and relief efforts. They need a robust and scalable platform to collect, process, and analyze data from various sources during emergency situations. Azure Logic Apps and Azure Functions enable the organization to create automated workflows that trigger actions in response to specific events. For example, they can automatically send alerts to first responders based on real-time sensor data or social media activity. In the retail industry, a chain of grocery stores wants to enhance customer loyalty and engagement. They implement a mobile app that offers personalized promotions and recommendations. Azure Cognitive Services, including Azure Cognitive Search and Azure Machine Learning, enable the app to analyze customer preferences and deliver tailored offers. The app's recommendation engine learns from user behavior *and continuously refines its suggestions. A media and entertainment company faces the challenge of managing and delivering content to a global audience. Azure Media Services and Azure Content Delivery Network (CDN) provide a scalable solution. They securely store and stream video content to viewers around the world, ensuring high-quality streaming and low latency. These real-world scenarios illustrate the versatility and impact of Azure's PaaS offerings. Organizations across various industries leverage Azure's capabilities to address their unique challenges, from scaling web applications and accelerating research to enhancing customer experiences and optimizing operations. By harnessing the power of Azure PaaS, these organizations drive innovation, improve efficiency, and achieve their business objectives in a rapidly evolving digital landscape.*

Chapter 6: Selecting the Right PaaS for Your Projects

IBM Cloud offers a comprehensive range of Platform as a Service (PaaS) offerings, designed to empower organizations in their journey towards building, deploying, and managing applications in a cloud-native and scalable manner. These PaaS services, hosted on the IBM Cloud platform, provide developers with the tools and resources needed to accelerate application development and reduce the complexities of infrastructure management. IBM Cloud PaaS offerings encompass various services, each tailored to address specific application development and deployment requirements. One of the central components of IBM Cloud's PaaS offerings is the IBM Cloud Foundry, a fully managed cloud application platform that simplifies the deployment and scaling of applications. Developers can leverage Cloud Foundry to build and deploy applications using various programming languages, including Java, Node.js, Python, and more. This platform abstracts away infrastructure concerns, allowing developers to focus solely on writing code and delivering features. IBM Cloud Kubernetes Service is another critical PaaS offering that caters to the growing adoption of containerization and microservices architectures. It provides a managed Kubernetes environment, simplifying the deployment, scaling, and management of containerized applications. Kubernetes offers orchestration capabilities that help developers automate container deployment, scaling, and load balancing. IBM Cloud Functions is IBM's serverless computing platform, enabling developers to build event-driven applications without the need to manage servers. Functions respond to events and run code snippets in response to triggers, making it an ideal choice for lightweight, event-based workloads. This serverless approach allows developers to focus on writing code and building applications without worrying about underlying infrastructure. IBM Cloud Databases offer a variety of managed database services, including IBM Db2 on Cloud, IBM Cloud Databases for PostgreSQL, and IBM Cloud Databases for MongoDB. These services cater to different database requirements, providing organizations with a choice of database engines for structured and unstructured data. With automatic scaling, backup, and high availability features, developers can efficiently manage their data without the burden of database administration. IBM Cloud Integration, powered by IBM App Connect, is a PaaS service that simplifies the integration of applications and data across cloud and on-premises environments. Developers can create integration flows to connect applications, systems, and data sources, enabling seamless data exchange and workflow automation. This service supports various connectors and standards, making it versatile for different integration needs. In the realm of artificial intelligence (AI) and machine learning (ML), IBM Cloud offers IBM Watson services, which include IBM Watson Assistant, Watson Discovery, Watson Language Translator, and more. These services *allow developers to infuse AI capabilities into their applications, enabling natural language understanding, sentiment analysis, and content discovery. IBM Watson services are particularly valuable for organizations looking to enhance customer experiences and gain insights from unstructured data. IBM Cloud Object Storage is a scalable and secure storage service that offers reliable object storage for a wide range of data types. It supports backup, archiving, and content distribution use cases, making it suitable for applications that require durable and cost-effective data storage. IBM Cloud offers a set of tools and services for DevOps and continuous delivery, such as IBM Cloud Continuous Delivery, which automates the deployment pipeline and accelerates the release of software updates. Developers can leverage these tools to streamline application development, testing, and deployment processes. Additionally, IBM Cloud Monitoring and Logging services provide real-time visibility into application performance and health, allowing organizations to proactively identify and resolve issues. IBM Cloud PaaS offerings are underpinned by a secure and compliant infrastructure. IBM Cloud adheres to industry-standard security practices and provides features like identity and access management (IAM), encryption at rest and in transit, and security monitoring and threat detection. Organizations in highly regulated industries, such as healthcare and finance, can rely on IBM Cloud's compliance certifications to meet their industry-specific requirements. IBM Cloud PaaS services also support multicloud and hybrid cloud strategies, allowing* organizations to integrate IBM Cloud with other cloud providers and on-premises environments seamlessly. This flexibility enables businesses to leverage the advantages of different cloud platforms while maintaining control over their data and applications. IBM Cloud PaaS offerings cater to a wide range of industries and use cases. For example, in the healthcare sector, IBM Cloud can support the development of secure and compliant healthcare applications that handle sensitive patient data. The platform provides the necessary tools and infrastructure to build and deploy healthcare solutions while meeting regulatory requirements, such as HIPAA. In the retail industry, organizations can leverage IBM Cloud PaaS services to develop and deploy e-commerce applications that scale to meet peak demand during sales events. The agility and scalability of the cloud platform allow retailers to deliver a seamless online shopping experience to customers. In the financial services sector, IBM Cloud PaaS offerings support the development of fintech applications that require high availability, security, and compliance. Organizations can use the platform's database services to manage financial data and leverage AI services for fraud detection and risk analysis. For startups and innovative enterprises, IBM Cloud provides a platform to rapidly prototype and deploy new applications and services. The ease of use and scalability of PaaS offerings enable organizations to experiment, iterate, and bring new ideas to market faster. IBM Cloud PaaS services also enable organizations to implement modern application architectures, such as microservices *and serverless computing. These architectures help businesses build resilient and highly scalable applications that can adapt to changing user demands. Overall, IBM Cloud PaaS services offer organizations the tools, infrastructure, and flexibility needed to accelerate application development, improve operational efficiency, and drive innovation across various industries and use cases.*

Chapter 7: Building and Deploying Applications on Paas

When selecting a Platform as a Service (Paas) provider for your organization, numerous factors must be carefully considered to ensure that the chosen platform aligns with your business needs and objectives. First and foremost, it is essential to assess your organization's specific requirements and goals. Understanding your application development and deployment needs, as well as your long-term strategic objectives, will help guide your choice of a PaaS provider that best fits your unique situation. Consider the programming languages and development tools your team is familiar with and prefers to use. Choosing a PaaS provider that supports the languages and tools your developers are already proficient in can significantly reduce the learning curve and accelerate development. Evaluate the scalability requirements of your applications. If your organization anticipates rapid growth or fluctuating workloads, selecting a PaaS provider with robust scaling capabilities is crucial to ensure your applications can handle increased demand without performance degradation. Additionally, assess the provider's pricing model, as unexpected costs can impact your budget. Determine whether the PaaS provider offers transparent and predictable pricing, as well as options for cost optimization, such as auto-scaling and resource utilization monitoring. Security considerations are paramount in today's digital landscape. Examine the security measures and compliance certifications offered by the PaaS provider to ensure that your applications and data will be adequately protected. Consider factors like data encryption, access controls, identity management, and compliance with industry-specific regulations. Evaluate the provider's data management and storage capabilities. If your applications require extensive data storage and management, choose a PaaS provider with robust database options, data analytics tools, and data backup and recovery features. Consider the provider's ecosystem and integration capabilities. Assess whether the PaaS platform integrates seamlessly with your existing tools, services, and third-party applications to minimize disruptions and streamline your development process. Look into the level of support and assistance provided by the PaaS provider. Consider factors like technical support, documentation, community forums, and training resources to ensure that your development team has access to the necessary guidance and assistance. Assess the provider's service-level agreements (SLAs) and uptime guarantees. Downtime can disrupt your operations and affect user experiences, so choosing a PaaS provider with a strong track record of uptime and reliable SLAs is crucial. Consider the geographic presence of the PaaS provider's data centers and regions. Selecting a provider with data centers in regions that align with your target audience or compliance requirements can enhance application performance and compliance. Evaluate the PaaS provider's disaster recovery and backup capabilities.

Ensure that the provider has robust disaster recovery mechanisms in place to safeguard your applications and data against unforeseen events. Assess the platform's monitoring and analytics features. Choose a PaaS provider that offers comprehensive monitoring, logging, and analytics tools to gain insights into your application's performance, identify bottlenecks, and troubleshoot issues effectively. Consider the level of vendor lock-in associated with the PaaS provider. Evaluate whether migrating your applications away from the platform would be feasible in the future, should your business requirements change. Assess the provider's track record and reputation in the industry. Research customer reviews, case studies, and testimonials to gain insights into the experiences of other organizations that have used the PaaS provider's services. Take into account the provider's commitment to innovation and staying current with emerging technologies. A forward-looking PaaS provider is more likely to offer features and services that align with future industry trends and technologies. Evaluate the provider's compliance with industry standards and certifications. For organizations operating in regulated industries, selecting a PaaS provider with relevant certifications, such as SOC 2 or ISO 27001, can simplify compliance efforts. Consider the level of customization and control the PaaS provider offers. Determine whether the platform allows you to configure resources, adjust settings, and customize your environment to meet your specific requirements. Assess the provider's ecosystem of add-ons, extensions, and marketplace offerings.

These additional services and integrations can enhance your application's functionality and save development time. Evaluate the PaaS provider's community and user base. A thriving community can provide valuable support, knowledge sharing, and resources for your development team. Consider the provider's track record in terms of service reliability and uptime. Look for historical performance data and uptime statistics to gauge the provider's reliability. Examine the provider's commitment to sustainability and environmental responsibility. For organizations with sustainability goals, choosing a PaaS provider with a strong environmental focus can align with your values. Assess the PaaS provider's data transfer and network capabilities. If your applications require high-speed data transfer or low-latency networking, verify that the provider's network infrastructure can meet your requirements. Consider the provider's pricing structure and billing options. Evaluate whether the provider offers pricing plans that align with your budget and cost expectations. Assess the level of automation and DevOps support provided by the PaaS platform. Automation features can streamline deployment, scaling, and management tasks, while DevOps support can enhance collaboration and efficiency. Evaluate the PaaS provider's commitment to data privacy and data sovereignty. For organizations with strict data privacy requirements, ensure that the provider adheres to relevant data protection regulations. Consider the level of flexibility and ease of migration offered by the PaaS provider. Determine whether you can easily migrate your existing applications and data to the platform without significant disruption. Assess the provider's commitment to ongoing updates and feature enhancements. Regular updates and improvements can keep your applications secure and up-to-date with the latest technologies. Ultimately, choosing the right PaaS provider for your organization requires a comprehensive evaluation of your specific needs and objectives, as well as a careful assessment of the provider's capabilities, security, support, and pricing. By considering these factors and conducting thorough research, you can make an informed decision that aligns with your organization's long-term success and growth.

Chapter 8: Best Practices for Scaling PaaS Environments

In the realm of Platform as a Service (PaaS), adhering to best practices is essential for successful application development and deployment. These best practices encompass a range of considerations and strategies that can help organizations harness the full potential of PaaS offerings. First and foremost, it is crucial to adopt a cloud-native mindset when developing applications on a PaaS platform. This entails designing applications with scalability, resilience, and flexibility in mind, taking full advantage of the cloud's capabilities. Leverage microservices architecture to break down applications into smaller, independently deployable components. This approach facilitates agility, as teams can develop and update microservices separately, minimizing disruption to the entire application. Additionally, containerization technologies, such as Docker, can enhance portability and consistency in deploying microservices across different environments. Implement continuous integration and continuous delivery (CI/CD) pipelines to automate the software development lifecycle. CI/CD pipelines streamline code integration, testing, and deployment, ensuring that changes are swiftly and reliably pushed to production. Leverage PaaS platform-native CI/CD tools or integrate with third-party solutions for efficient pipeline management. Adopt a serverless computing model for specific workloads and functions. Serverless platforms, like AWS Lambda or Azure Functions, enable event-driven, cost-effective execution of code without the need to manage servers. This model is particularly suited for tasks such as data processing, real-time analytics, and automation. Embrace a DevOps culture that promotes collaboration between development and operations teams. By fostering a culture of shared responsibility, organizations can achieve faster deployment, improved quality, and enhanced feedback loops. Automate infrastructure provisioning and management using infrastructure as code (IaC) tools. IaC enables the definition and deployment of infrastructure resources through code, ensuring consistency and repeatability in infrastructure setup. Implement robust monitoring and observability practices to gain real-time insights into application performance and health. Leverage monitoring tools and techniques to track metrics, detect anomalies, and troubleshoot issues promptly. Consider using application performance management (APM) solutions to gain deeper visibility into application behavior. Adopt a multi-cloud or hybrid cloud strategy for increased resilience and redundancy. By distributing applications and data across multiple cloud providers or combining on-premises resources with the cloud, organizations can mitigate the risk of downtime and data loss. Prioritize security from the outset of application development. Implement security best practices, such as encryption, access controls, and vulnerability assessments, to safeguard sensitive data and applications. Leverage identity and access management (IAM) solutions to enforce granular access policies and authentication. Regularly update dependencies and libraries to address security vulnerabilities and maintain a secure application stack. Implement data backup and disaster recovery plans to ensure data resilience and business continuity. Regularly test and validate backup and recovery processes to minimize downtime and data loss in the event of a disaster. Adhere to compliance standards and regulations applicable to your industry. Ensure that your PaaS applications comply with data protection, privacy, and industry-specific regulations. Consider utilizing PaaS platform-native services for data storage, which often include built-in compliance features. Optimize resource utilization and cost management by regularly reviewing resource allocation and scaling policies. Scale resources based on actual usage and demand to avoid overprovisioning or underutilization. Leverage auto-scaling features provided by PaaS platforms to automatically adjust resources as needed. Implement caching mechanisms and content delivery networks (CDNs) to enhance application performance and reduce latency. Caching frequently accessed data and distributing content through CDNs can improve user experiences and reduce server load. Ensure thorough testing and quality assurance (QA) processes are in place. Implement automated testing, including unit testing, integration testing, and performance testing, to identify and rectify issues early in the development process. Implement version control and versioning strategies for code and configurations. Maintaining a clear history of changes and versions helps track and manage code evolution and simplifies rollback procedures if necessary. Prioritize documentation and knowledge sharing among team members. Well-documented code, architectural diagrams, and development guidelines enhance collaboration and facilitate onboarding of new team members. Leverage collaboration and communication tools for effective team coordination. Using collaboration platforms and communication channels helps geographically distributed teams collaborate seamlessly. Consider adopting agile and iterative development methodologies. Agile practices, such as Scrum or Kanban, promote iterative development, frequent feedback, and adaptability to changing requirements. Implement robust error handling and recovery mechanisms to ensure application resilience. Plan for scenarios where errors or failures may occur and define strategies for graceful degradation and recovery. Adopt a culture of continuous improvement and learning. Encourage teams to regularly reflect on their processes and outcomes, seeking ways to optimize and enhance their development practices. Invest in ongoing training and skill development to stay current with emerging technologies and best practices. Consider leveraging managed services provided by the PaaS platform. PaaS platforms often offer a variety of managed services, such as databases, caching, and authentication, which can simplify application development and maintenance. Leverage these services to offload operational overhead and focus on application logic. Regularly review and update your application architecture to align with evolving business needs and technology trends. Consider architectural patterns, such as event-driven architectures or microservices, that can help your applications scale and evolve gracefully. In summary, PaaS application development best practices encompass a wide range of strategies and considerations that can enhance the efficiency, scalability, security, and reliability of applications deployed on PaaS platforms. By adopting cloud-native approaches, embracing automation, prioritizing security, and fostering a culture of collaboration and continuous improvement, organizations can leverage the full potential of PaaS offerings to drive innovation and achieve their business objectives in a rapidly evolving digital landscape.

Chapter 9: Ensuring Security and Compliance in PaaS

Scaling strategies for Platform as a Service (PaaS) applications are critical for ensuring that your applications can handle increased workloads and traffic without performance degradation or downtime. Scaling involves the allocation of additional resources, such as computing power, memory, or storage, to meet the demands of your application. One of the primary scaling strategies for PaaS applications is horizontal scaling, also known as scaling out. Horizontal scaling involves adding more instances or copies of your application to distribute the load evenly. This strategy is particularly effective for stateless applications that can easily handle traffic distribution across multiple instances. When your application experiences increased demand, you can provision additional instances to share the load and maintain optimal performance. Horizontal scaling provides flexibility and can be automated to respond to changing traffic patterns. Another scaling strategy is vertical scaling, also known as scaling up. Vertical scaling involves increasing the capacity of individual instances by adding more resources, such as CPU cores or memory. This strategy is suitable for applications that benefit from increased processing power or memory capacity. Vertical scaling can be achieved by upgrading the hardware or changing the instance type of your PaaS platform. It is essential to monitor your application's performance and resource utilization to determine when vertical scaling is necessary. Auto-scaling is a dynamic scaling strategy that automatically adjusts the number of application instances based on predefined conditions. Auto-scaling policies can be set to trigger instance scaling when specific thresholds, such as CPU usage or request rate, are exceeded. This strategy allows your application to adapt to varying workloads without manual intervention, ensuring efficient resource utilization. Load balancing is a crucial component of scaling strategies for PaaS applications. Load balancers distribute incoming traffic across multiple instances to ensure that no single instance becomes overwhelmed. This approach enhances application availability, scalability, and fault tolerance. Load balancers can be configured to use various algorithms, such as round-robin or least connections, to distribute traffic. Content delivery networks (CDNs) are valuable for scaling applications with geographically distributed users. CDNs cache and deliver content from edge locations closer to the end-users, reducing latency and offloading the origin server. By leveraging a CDN, you can ensure that your application performs well for users worldwide. Caching is another scaling technique that involves storing frequently accessed data in memory or a cache store. Caching reduces the need to retrieve data from the database or backend services for every request, improving response times and reducing the load on your application. Caching solutions, such as Redis or Memcached, can be integrated into your PaaS application to enhance performance. Database scaling is a critical consideration for applications that rely on databases to store and retrieve data. Scaling databases can be achieved through various methods, including vertical scaling, sharding, and replication. Vertical scaling involves increasing the resources allocated to the database server, while sharding divides the data across multiple database instances. Replication replicates data to multiple database servers to ensure availability and load distribution. Database as a Service (DBaaS) offerings in PaaS platforms can simplify database scaling and management. Serverless computing is an innovative scaling strategy that allows your application to run code in response to specific events without the need to manage servers. Serverless platforms, such as AWS Lambda or Azure Functions, automatically allocate resources as needed to execute code snippets. This approach is cost-effective and ideal for event-driven workloads. Containerization and container orchestration platforms, like Docker and Kubernetes, offer efficient scaling strategies for microservices-based applications. Containers provide a lightweight and consistent runtime environment for applications, while orchestration tools enable automated scaling and management of containerized services. These platforms facilitate rapid scaling and deployment of microservices. Monitoring and analytics play a crucial role in scaling strategies for PaaS applications. Monitoring tools provide insights into application performance, resource utilization, and traffic patterns. By analyzing these metrics, you can make informed decisions about when and how to scale your application. Application performance management (APM) solutions offer comprehensive monitoring and diagnostics capabilities. Testing is essential to validate the effectiveness of your scaling strategies. Load testing, stress testing, and performance testing simulate various traffic scenarios to evaluate how well your application scales under different conditions. Testing helps identify potential bottlenecks and areas for improvement in your scaling architecture. Scaling should be a proactive and anticipatory process rather than a reactive one. By regularly analyzing performance data and defining scaling policies based on anticipated traffic patterns, you can ensure that your application scales smoothly without service interruptions. Failover and redundancy are vital components of scaling strategies to enhance application availability. Redundant instances and failover mechanisms ensure that if one instance or component fails, traffic is routed to healthy instances. This strategy minimizes downtime and provides fault tolerance. Elasticity is a key principle in scaling strategies for PaaS applications. Elasticity allows your application to scale up or down in response to changes in demand. It ensures that you allocate resources efficiently, avoiding over-provisioning or underutilization. Scalability is a crucial consideration when selecting a PaaS platform. Choose a platform that offers the scalability features and options that align with your application's requirements. Ultimately, scaling strategies for PaaS applications are essential for meeting the demands of a dynamic and evolving digital landscape. By implementing horizontal and vertical scaling, auto-scaling, load balancing, CDNs, caching, and other techniques, you can ensure that your PaaS applications deliver high performance, availability, and responsiveness to users while optimizing resource utilization and cost-effectiveness.

Chapter 10: The Future of PaaS and Cloud Computing: Trends and Innovations

Security measures for Platform as a Service (PaaS) environments are of paramount importance to protect applications, data, and infrastructure in the cloud. PaaS platforms provide a range of tools and services to facilitate application development and deployment, but security remains a shared responsibility between the cloud provider and the user. One fundamental aspect of PaaS security is identity and access management (IAM). IAM solutions enable organizations to control user access to resources, ensuring that only authorized individuals can interact with applications and data. Implementing strong authentication methods, such as multi-factor authentication (MFA), enhances access security. Role-based access control (RBAC) allows organizations to assign granular permissions to users and restrict access based on job roles and responsibilities. Encryption plays a pivotal role in securing data in transit and at rest within PaaS environments. Transport Layer Security (TLS) ensures that data transmitted between clients and PaaS services is encrypted, preventing eavesdropping and tampering. Data encryption at rest safeguards data stored in databases, storage services, and backups. PaaS platforms often provide encryption mechanisms and key management services to simplify encryption implementation. Network security is a critical consideration in PaaS environments. Virtual private clouds (VPCs) or virtual networks enable organizations to isolate their PaaS resources from the public internet, reducing exposure to threats. Network security groups (NSGs) or security group policies allow fine-grained control over inbound and outbound traffic, limiting communication to trusted sources. Web application firewalls (WAFs) protect applications from common web-based attacks, such as SQL injection and cross-site scripting (XSS). Distributed denial-of-service (DDoS) protection services help mitigate and absorb volumetric attacks, ensuring application availability. Regularly patching and updating PaaS resources is essential to address vulnerabilities and security patches promptly. PaaS providers often manage the underlying infrastructure, including patching, but users are responsible for keeping their applications and configurations up to date. Implementing a vulnerability management program helps organizations identify and remediate security flaws in their PaaS environments. Security information and event management (SIEM) solutions, integrated with PaaS platforms, provide real-time threat detection and incident response capabilities. SIEM tools collect and analyze log data from PaaS services, enabling organizations to detect anomalies and security incidents. Implementing intrusion detection and prevention systems (IDS/IPS) adds an additional layer of security by monitoring network traffic for malicious activity and blocking potential threats. Container security is crucial in PaaS environments that use containerization technologies like Docker and

Kubernetes. Organizations should scan container images for vulnerabilities, enforce access controls, and regularly update containers to address security issues. Runtime security solutions protect containers from runtime threats and provide visibility into container behavior. Compliance and regulatory requirements vary across industries and regions. PaaS platforms often offer compliance certifications and documentation to help organizations meet their specific compliance needs. Organizations should understand their compliance obligations and leverage PaaS features that support compliance, such as audit logs and data encryption. Data protection is a critical aspect of PaaS security. Organizations should classify data and implement data retention policies to safeguard sensitive information. Data encryption, both in transit and at rest, helps protect data from unauthorized access. Backup and disaster recovery strategies ensure data resilience in case of unexpected incidents or data loss. Organizations should regularly back up their PaaS resources and test data recovery procedures. Security monitoring and incident response are essential components of a robust security strategy. Continuous monitoring of PaaS resources and applications allows organizations to detect security incidents and anomalies promptly. Incident response plans outline the actions to take in the event of a security breach or incident. Security teams should conduct regular security assessments and penetration testing to identify vulnerabilities and weaknesses in their PaaS environments. Implementing secure coding practices is critical for PaaS application development. Developers should be trained in secure coding techniques and follow best practices to prevent common vulnerabilities like injection attacks and insecure deserialization. Static and dynamic code analysis tools can help identify security issues during development and testing phases. Container security practices, such as scanning for vulnerabilities and configuring security settings, are also essential for containerized applications. Data encryption and tokenization techniques should be employed to protect sensitive data within PaaS applications. Security automation and orchestration can help organizations streamline security tasks and responses. Implementing automated security policies and workflows can reduce the risk of human error and ensure consistent security enforcement. Security incident response automation can expedite threat detection and mitigation. Security awareness and training programs should be established to educate users and staff about security best practices and the potential risks associated with PaaS environments. Employees should be aware of phishing threats, social engineering attacks, and other security challenges. PaaS platforms often provide security-related features and services that organizations can leverage to enhance their security posture. These include security dashboards, threat detection tools, and integration with third-party security solutions. Security information sharing and collaboration with other organizations and security communities can help stay informed about emerging threats and vulnerabilities. By sharing threat intelligence and best practices, *organizations can collectively improve their security defenses. Regular security audits and assessments can help organizations evaluate and validate their PaaS security controls. External security audits and third-party assessments provide an objective view of the security posture. Organizations should address audit findings and recommendations promptly to improve security. Incident response exercises and tabletop simulations allow organizations to practice their response procedures and identify areas for improvement. Regular testing and evaluation of incident response plans help ensure readiness in the event of a security incident. PaaS security is an ongoing process that requires vigilance and adaptation to evolving threats and technologies. Organizations should stay informed about the latest security trends, vulnerabilities, and best practices in the PaaS landscape. Collaboration with security experts and organizations in the same industry can provide valuable insights and guidance. Ultimately, a multi-layered approach to security, encompassing identity and access management, encryption, network security, compliance, data protection, and monitoring, is essential to safeguard PaaS environments and the applications they host. By implementing a comprehensive security strategy and staying proactive in the face of emerging threats, organizations can confidently harness the benefits of PaaS while minimizing security risks. Emerging trends in Platform as a Service (PaaS) are reshaping the landscape of application development and deployment, offering new possibilities and opportunities for organizations. One of the prominent trends in PaaS is the rise of serverless computing, which allows developers to focus solely on writing code without managing servers. Serverless platforms, such as AWS Lambda and Azure Functions, automatically scale resources and charge users based on actual usage, promoting cost efficiency and rapid development. Microservices architecture is gaining traction in PaaS environments as organizations seek to break down monolithic applications into smaller, manageable components. Microservices enable agility, scalability, and independent deployment of application modules, enhancing flexibility and reducing development bottlenecks. Kubernetes, an open-source container orchestration platform, has become a key enabler of containerization and microservices adoption in PaaS. Kubernetes provides automated container management, scaling, and load balancing, making it easier to deploy and manage containerized applications in PaaS environments. Multi-cloud and hybrid cloud strategies are becoming increasingly prevalent as organizations aim to leverage multiple cloud providers or combine on-premises resources with the cloud. These strategies offer flexibility, resilience, and redundancy, reducing the risk of vendor lock-in and enhancing business continuity. Edge computing is emerging as a vital trend in PaaS, enabling data processing and computation closer to the data source. Edge platforms facilitate real-time data analysis, low-latency responses, and reduced data transfer to centralized cloud data centers. Artificial intelligence (AI) and machine learning (ML) are being integrated into PaaS platforms, providing developers with access to AI and ML services for data analysis, natural language processing, and predictive modeling. These capabilities enhance the functionality and intelligence of PaaS applications. Blockchain technology is finding its way into PaaS for secure and transparent transactions and data sharing. PaaS offerings are incorporating blockchain services to enable applications that require trust, immutability, and decentralized consensus. DevOps and DevSecOps practices continue to evolve in PaaS environments, emphasizing collaboration, automation, and security throughout the software development lifecycle. DevOps tools and practices enable faster development cycles, reduced errors, and improved application quality. Serverless containerization is a hybrid approach that combines the benefits of serverless computing and containers. This trend allows developers to deploy containerized applications in serverless platforms, combining the advantages of both paradigms. Integration of PaaS with Internet of Things (IoT) platforms is facilitating the development of IoT applications and solutions. PaaS offerings provide IoT developers with tools and services for data processing, device management, and real-time analytics. Low-code and no-code development platforms are gaining popularity in PaaS, enabling users with varying levels of technical expertise to build applications with minimal coding. These platforms accelerate application development and reduce the skills gap. Container security and Kubernetes security are paramount concerns as containerization and orchestration become* integral to PaaS. Security solutions and best practices are evolving to protect containerized applications and their environments. Quantum computing is an emerging trend with the potential to revolutionize PaaS. Quantum PaaS platforms are beginning to provide access to quantum computing resources for solving complex problems in fields like cryptography, optimization, and materials science. Edge AI, which combines edge computing with artificial intelligence, allows for real-time AI processing at the edge of the network. This trend enables applications with low-latency AI capabilities, such as autonomous vehicles and industrial automation. PaaS providers are increasingly focusing on environmental sustainability and green computing. Efforts to reduce energy consumption, carbon emissions, and resource usage align with the growing emphasis on sustainability in the technology industry. Hybrid PaaS platforms are gaining traction, allowing organizations to seamlessly manage and deploy applications across on-premises and cloud environments. These platforms offer consistency and flexibility in hybrid cloud deployments. Enhanced observability and monitoring tools are essential in complex PaaS environments. PaaS providers are offering advanced monitoring and APM (Application Performance Management) solutions to gain insights into application behavior and performance. PaaS offerings are expanding beyond traditional application hosting to include data analytics, data warehousing, and data processing services. These capabilities empower organizations to extract valuable insights from their data. Security and compliance automation are *becoming integral to PaaS, streamlining security and compliance management tasks through automation. This trend helps organizations meet regulatory requirements and protect their PaaS environments. Natural language processing (NLP) and conversational AI are being integrated into PaaS platforms to enable voice and text-based interactions in applications. Chatbots and virtual assistants are examples of NLP-powered applications. Container-native development platforms are emerging, offering tools and workflows designed specifically for building and deploying containerized applications. These platforms simplify the development and management of containerized workloads. AI-driven automation is enhancing PaaS operations, with AI-powered tools automating tasks like resource provisioning, scaling, and troubleshooting. AI-driven automation improves efficiency and reduces manual intervention. Blockchain-based smart contracts are finding applications in PaaS, enabling automated, self-executing agreements and transactions. Smart contracts enhance trust and transparency in PaaS applications. Quantum-resistant cryptography is a growing concern as quantum computing advances. PaaS providers are exploring post-quantum cryptography solutions to safeguard data and communications from future quantum threats. Interoperability and standards in PaaS are gaining attention as organizations seek to avoid vendor lock-in and ensure compatibility between PaaS services and tools. Open standards and initiatives promote interoperability in the PaaS ecosystem. Ethical AI and responsible AI practices are becoming essential in*

PaaS, addressing concerns related to bias, fairness, transparency, and accountability in AI algorithms and applications. Data privacy regulations, such as GDPR and CCPA, are shaping PaaS services, with providers offering tools and features to help organizations comply with data protection laws. Edge-native development platforms are catering to the unique requirements of edge computing, offering specialized tools for developing edge applications. Edge-native platforms focus on low-latency, real-time processing at the edge of the network. PaaS ecosystems are expanding to include industry-specific solutions and vertical integration, addressing the specific needs of sectors like healthcare, finance, and manufacturing. This trend enables organizations to leverage PaaS for industry-specific applications and compliance. Quantum machine learning (QML) is an emerging field that combines quantum computing and machine learning to solve complex problems with quantum algorithms. QML holds promise for applications in optimization, drug discovery, and materials science. Ethical considerations in AI, such as transparency, explainability, and fairness, are influencing the development of AI-powered PaaS applications. Organizations are increasingly incorporating ethical AI principles into their PaaS projects. Zero-trust security models are gaining prominence in PaaS environments, emphasizing the need for continuous verification and strict access controls to mitigate security risks. Zero-trust approaches enhance security in PaaS applications and networks. Edge-native AI combines the capabilities of edge computing and artificial intelligence to deliver AI-powered insights and actions at the edge. This trend enables real-time AI processing in remote and resource-constrained environments. Blockchain consortiums and partnerships are forming to create industry-specific blockchain networks and platforms. Collaborative efforts aim to address industry challenges and enable blockchain adoption in PaaS. PaaS providers are investing in quantum computing research and development, exploring quantum PaaS offerings and services. Quantum PaaS has the potential to revolutionize industries through quantum algorithms and computing power. The evolution of PaaS is shaped by the convergence of these emerging trends, driven by the demand for innovation, efficiency, security, and sustainability in the rapidly evolving digital landscape. As organizations continue to explore and adopt PaaS solutions, staying informed about these trends is essential to make informed decisions and leverage the full potential of PaaS for their applications and businesses.

BOOK 4
From Novice to Pro
PaaS Mastery Across Azure Pipelines, Google Cloud, Microsoft Azure, and IBM Cloud

ROB BOTWRIGHT

Chapter 1: Introduction to Platform as a Service (PaaS)

Platform as a Service, commonly referred to as PaaS, is a fundamental concept in the realm of cloud computing that has revolutionized the way applications are developed, deployed, and managed. At its core, PaaS is a cloud service model that provides a platform and environment for developers to build, test, and deploy applications without the complexity of managing underlying infrastructure. It abstracts away the intricacies of hardware provisioning, operating system management, and network configurations, allowing developers to focus solely on coding and application logic. The concept of PaaS emerged as a natural progression in the evolution of cloud computing, building upon the foundations laid by Infrastructure as a Service (IaaS) and Software as a Service (SaaS) models. While IaaS offers virtualized computing resources like virtual machines and storage, and SaaS delivers fully-fledged applications over the internet, PaaS strikes a balance between the two by offering a platform for application development and deployment. One of the defining characteristics of PaaS is its versatility, as it supports a wide range of programming languages, frameworks, and tools, enabling developers to work with the technologies they are most comfortable with. PaaS platforms typically provide a comprehensive set of services and tools that streamline the development lifecycle, from code creation to deployment and scaling. These services encompass databases, development frameworks, middleware, and more, all integrated into a cohesive environment. In essence, PaaS acts as a facilitator, empowering developers to bring their ideas to life efficiently and rapidly. One of the key advantages of PaaS is its scalability, which allows applications to grow seamlessly in response to increasing demand. PaaS providers offer dynamic scaling capabilities, automatically adjusting resources to match the workload, ensuring optimal performance and cost-efficiency. This ability to scale horizontally and vertically is a crucial factor for businesses that experience fluctuating traffic patterns and demand spikes. Another pivotal aspect of PaaS is its focus on collaboration and teamwork. PaaS platforms often include collaborative tools and features that enable multiple developers to work together on the same project, promoting efficiency and code consistency. Version control, code repositories, and continuous integration/continuous deployment (CI/CD) pipelines are integral components of the PaaS ecosystem, fostering a culture of collaboration and DevOps practices. Security is a paramount concern in cloud computing, and PaaS is no exception. PaaS providers invest heavily in security measures to protect data, applications, and infrastructure. They implement robust access controls, encryption mechanisms, and compliance certifications to ensure the confidentiality and integrity of sensitive information. Furthermore, PaaS platforms offer automated security updates and patches to shield applications from emerging threats. For businesses, PaaS offers significant cost savings compared to traditional on-premises infrastructure. It eliminates the need for upfront capital expenditure on hardware and software, replacing it with a pay-as-you-go model, where organizations only pay for the resources and services they consume. This cost-efficient approach is particularly appealing for startups and small to medium-sized enterprises (SMEs) looking to minimize financial barriers to entry. The concept of PaaS also facilitates rapid prototyping and experimentation. Developers can quickly spin up development environments, test new ideas, and iterate on projects without being encumbered by infrastructure setup and configuration. This agility accelerates the innovation cycle and empowers businesses to adapt to changing market conditions swiftly. Vendor lock-in is a common concern in cloud computing, but PaaS providers are keenly aware of this issue. To address it, many PaaS platforms adhere to open standards and interoperability, enabling applications and data to be easily transferred between different cloud providers or back to on-premises environments. This portability provides businesses with flexibility and mitigates the risks associated with vendor dependence. Additionally, PaaS often integrates with existing tools and services, allowing organizations to leverage their investments in software and systems. One of the driving forces behind the adoption of PaaS is the democratization of technology. It levels the playing field, giving small startups and developers access to the same sophisticated tools and resources that were once the exclusive domain of large enterprises. This democratization has led to a proliferation of innovative applications and services, disrupting industries and spurring digital transformation. PaaS also plays a pivotal role in supporting modern application development paradigms, such as microservices and containerization. These approaches emphasize breaking applications into smaller, loosely coupled components, which can be *independently developed, deployed, and scaled. PaaS platforms often provide native support for container orchestration tools like Kubernetes, making it easier to manage containerized applications. Moreover, PaaS fosters a culture of continuous innovation and improvement. With the ability to automate the deployment pipeline and leverage tools for monitoring and analytics, organizations can gather insights into application performance and user behavior. This data-driven approach enables iterative development and refinement, ensuring that applications meet evolving user needs. In summary, the concept of Platform as a Service (PaaS) represents a significant paradigm shift in cloud computing, empowering developers and organizations to build and deploy applications with unprecedented ease and efficiency. It encapsulates the principles of abstraction, collaboration, scalability, cost-efficiency, security, and innovation, making it a vital enabler of digital transformation and a key driver of the modern software development landscape. As technology continues to evolve, PaaS will undoubtedly evolve with it, offering even more sophisticated tools and services to meet the demands of an ever-changing digital world. For businesses and developers, embracing PaaS is not just a choice; it is an imperative step in staying competitive and agile in the fast-paced realm of cloud computing. To truly understand the concept of Platform as a Service (PaaS) and its significance in the world of technology, it is essential to delve into its historical perspective and trace its evolution over time. The roots of PaaS can be traced back to the early days of computing, where developers had to create applications that were tightly coupled with the* underlying hardware and operating systems. During this era, each application was built to run on a specific hardware platform, making it challenging to port software to different systems. As the computing landscape evolved, the need for a more flexible and portable approach to application development became apparent. The emergence of virtualization technologies in the early 2000s marked a significant milestone in the evolution of PaaS. Virtualization allowed multiple virtual machines to run on a single physical server, effectively decoupling applications from the underlying hardware. This newfound flexibility paved the way for the development of Infrastructure as a Service (IaaS), where users could provision virtualized resources like virtual machines, storage, and networking on-demand. While IaaS offered improved resource management and scalability, developers were still burdened with many of the tasks associated with configuring and managing the operating system and runtime environments. It became evident that there was a need for a higher-level abstraction that could further simplify the development and deployment of applications. This need gave rise to the concept of PaaS, which aimed to provide developers with a fully managed platform for building and running applications. One of the early pioneers of PaaS was Google App Engine, launched in 2008, which allowed developers to build web applications using popular programming languages like Python and Java without worrying about the underlying infrastructure. Google App Engine introduced the idea of serverless computing, where developers could focus solely on writing code, and the platform would automatically manage the runtime environment, scaling, and infrastructure. Around *the same time, other cloud providers, including Microsoft with Azure and Salesforce with Force.com, began offering their versions of PaaS platforms. These platforms offered a range of services, including databases, middleware, and development tools, to simplify application development and deployment. The introduction of PaaS was a game-changer for developers and businesses alike. It abstracted away the complexities of infrastructure management, allowing developers to concentrate on writing code and building applications. Developers no longer needed to worry about provisioning servers, configuring operating systems, or managing networking—tasks that had traditionally consumed a significant amount of their time and effort. PaaS platforms offered a range of services that could be easily integrated into applications, such as databases, identity management, and messaging services. This integration allowed developers to leverage pre-built components, reducing development time and effort. Moreover, PaaS introduced the concept of auto-scaling, where the platform automatically adjusted the number of application instances to handle changes in traffic. This scalability feature ensured that applications could efficiently handle varying workloads, from low traffic periods to sudden spikes in demand. As PaaS continued to evolve, it began to support a broader array of programming languages and frameworks, catering to the diverse needs of developers. This flexibility meant that developers could use their preferred tools and languages, further streamlining the development process. The adoption of microservices architecture also played a crucial role in shaping the evolution of PaaS. Microservices encouraged the decomposition of monolithic applications into smaller, independently deployable services. PaaS platforms embraced this architectural shift, providing tools for managing and orchestrating containerized microservices. This shift allowed organizations to build more scalable, resilient, and maintainable applications. In recent years, serverless computing has emerged as a significant advancement in the PaaS landscape. Serverless platforms, such as AWS Lambda and Azure Functions, take the concept of abstraction to the next level. Developers no longer need to worry about provisioning virtual machines or containers; they can write individual functions or code snippets that are executed in response to specific events or triggers. Serverless platforms handle all the underlying infrastructure, including scaling, automatically. This serverless paradigm has become a game-changer for certain use cases, particularly for event-driven and highly scalable applications. The adoption of containers and container orchestration platforms, like Docker and Kubernetes, has also influenced the evolution of PaaS. Many PaaS providers have integrated container support, enabling developers to build, deploy, and manage containerized applications directly within the platform. This integration has allowed organizations to embrace containerization and microservices while benefiting from the convenience of PaaS. Moreover, PaaS platforms have evolved to support hybrid cloud and multi-cloud deployments. This flexibility enables organizations to run their applications seamlessly across on-premises data centers and multiple cloud providers. It reduces vendor lock-in and provides greater control over where and how applications are deployed. Security and compliance have been at the forefront of PaaS evolution. As businesses entrust their critical data and applications to the cloud, PaaS providers have invested heavily in robust security measures. They offer encryption, identity and access management, compliance certifications, and threat detection services to safeguard sensitive information. The historical perspective and evolution of PaaS reflect the growing demand for simplification, agility, scalability, and cost-efficiency in application development and deployment. PaaS has emerged as a transformative force, empowering developers to innovate rapidly while providing organizations with the tools and platforms they need to thrive in an increasingly digital world. From its early days as a concept to its current state as a cornerstone of cloud computing, PaaS continues to evolve, offering new possibilities and opportunities for the future of application development.*

Chapter 2: Getting Started with Azure Pipelines

Setting up your Azure DevOps environment is a crucial step in establishing a robust and efficient development pipeline for your software projects. Azure DevOps, formerly known as Visual Studio Team Services (VSTS) and Team Foundation Server (TFS), is a comprehensive set of development tools and services provided by Microsoft to facilitate the entire software development lifecycle. To begin setting up your Azure DevOps environment, you first need to create an Azure DevOps organization, which serves as the central hub for your projects, teams, and repositories. You can sign up for Azure DevOps and choose from a range of pricing plans, including free options with certain limitations. Once you've created your organization, you can start defining the structure of your projects by creating individual projects or grouping related projects under a common umbrella. Projects in Azure DevOps help you organize your work and resources effectively. For each project, you can define teams, repositories, boards, pipelines, and other resources tailored to your specific development needs. Next, you'll want to configure version control for your project by creating a Git repository or selecting a version control system that suits your project's requirements. Azure DevOps offers native support for Git, providing robust version control capabilities and branching strategies to manage your codebase. Once your repository is set up, you can clone it to your local development environment using Git tools or integrated development environments (IDEs) like Visual Studio, Visual Studio Code, or others. This allows you to work on your code locally and collaborate with other team members through commits, branches, and pull requests. To streamline the development process further, you can configure build and release pipelines in Azure DevOps. Build pipelines automate the compilation, testing, and packaging of your code, ensuring that your application is consistently built and tested as changes are pushed to the repository. Release pipelines automate the deployment of your application to various environments, such as development, staging, and production, with each environment tailored to your specific requirements. Azure DevOps provides a wide range of build and release tasks and integrations with various deployment targets, including Azure services, on-premises servers, and other cloud providers. You can customize your pipelines to meet your project's specific needs, including running tests, executing scripts, and managing dependencies. Integrating automated testing into your pipelines is a crucial step in ensuring the quality of your software. Azure DevOps supports various testing frameworks and tools, allowing you to execute unit tests, integration tests, and UI tests as part of your build and release pipelines. By incorporating testing into your pipelines, you can catch issues early in the development process and deliver high-quality software to your users. Continuous integration (CI) and continuous delivery (CD) are key principles in modern software development. Azure DevOps makes it easy to implement CI/CD pipelines, ensuring that code changes are automatically built, tested, and deployed to production as they are committed. This reduces manual interventions, accelerates the release cycle, and minimizes the risk of errors during deployment. To enhance collaboration and communication within your development teams, you can set up work tracking and project management tools in Azure DevOps. Azure Boards offer features like backlogs, sprint planning, and kanban boards to help teams manage their work effectively and visualize project progress. You can create user stories, bugs, tasks, and other work items to track and prioritize your team's efforts. Assign work items to team members, set due dates, and define dependencies to streamline the development process. Azure DevOps also provides robust reporting and analytics capabilities, allowing you to track project metrics, monitor team performance, and gain insights into the health of your software projects. You can create customized dashboards and reports to visualize data and make informed decisions. Azure DevOps integrates with a wide range of development tools and third-party services to extend its capabilities and meet your specific needs. You can connect Azure DevOps to your favorite code repositories, issue trackers, testing tools, and collaboration platforms. This integration ecosystem allows you to leverage your existing tools and workflows while benefiting from the power and flexibility of Azure DevOps. Security is a critical aspect of setting up your Azure DevOps environment. You can configure role-based access control (RBAC) to define who can access specific resources and perform actions within your organization. Azure DevOps provides predefined security roles and allows you to create custom roles to align with your organization's security policies. Additionally, you can enable features like multi-factor authentication (MFA) to enhance the security of user accounts. To safeguard your source code and artifacts, Azure DevOps offers features like branch policies, code review workflows, and artifact retention policies. These controls help maintain code quality, prevent unauthorized changes, and ensure the availability of necessary artifacts. Backup and disaster recovery plans are essential aspects of setting up your Azure DevOps environment. Azure DevOps provides automated backup and restore capabilities to protect your data and configurations. By regularly backing up your organization's data, you can recover from unexpected data loss or disruptions quickly. For added resilience, you can also replicate your Azure DevOps data across multiple geographic regions to ensure availability even in the face of regional outages. Setting up your Azure DevOps environment also includes defining governance policies and compliance measures. You can enforce policies related to code quality, security scanning, and deployment controls to ensure that your applications meet your organization's standards and regulatory requirements. Azure DevOps allows you to integrate with Azure Policy and Azure Blueprints for comprehensive governance and compliance management. Another critical aspect of your Azure DevOps environment setup is documentation and *knowledge sharing. You can create and maintain documentation within Azure DevOps using Wiki, which offers collaborative editing and versioning capabilities. This helps capture important information, best practices, and project-specific knowledge to facilitate onboarding and knowledge transfer. Lastly, continuous improvement is a fundamental principle of setting up your Azure DevOps environment. Regularly review and refine your pipelines, processes, and configurations to optimize your development workflow continually. Leverage Azure DevOps Analytics to gain insights into your team's performance and identify areas for improvement. By embracing a culture of continuous improvement, you can enhance the efficiency, quality, and agility of your software development projects. In summary, setting up your Azure DevOps environment is a comprehensive process that encompasses various aspects of software development and project management. It begins with the creation of an Azure DevOps organization, project structuring, version control, and local development setup. From there, you configure build and release pipelines, automated testing, work tracking, and project management tools. Security, backup, governance, and documentation are essential considerations for a robust environment. Ultimately, your Azure DevOps environment should be adaptable and continuously improved to meet the evolving needs of your organization and projects. By carefully planning and configuring your Azure DevOps environment, you can establish a solid foundation for successful software development and delivery.*

Chapter 3: Mastering Google Cloud Platform (GCP) PaaS Services

Google Cloud Platform (GCP) offers a wide array of Platform as a Service (PaaS) offerings designed to simplify application development and deployment. These PaaS offerings are a fundamental part of GCP's cloud services ecosystem, enabling developers to focus on writing code rather than managing infrastructure. GCP's PaaS offerings cover a broad spectrum of use cases, from web and mobile application development to data analytics and machine learning. One of the core PaaS services provided by GCP is Google App Engine, a fully managed platform for building and deploying web applications and APIs. Google App Engine abstracts away infrastructure management tasks, allowing developers to write code in Python, Java, Node.js, Ruby, Go, or PHP and deploy it with ease. App Engine automatically handles tasks like scaling, load balancing, and health monitoring, ensuring that applications run smoothly even under heavy traffic. App Engine supports both standard and flexible environments, offering flexibility in choosing the runtime that best suits your application's needs. GCP's Cloud Functions is another PaaS offering that enables serverless computing. With Cloud Functions, developers can write single-purpose functions in languages like Node.js, Python, Go, and Java and execute them in response to events or HTTP requests. This serverless approach allows developers to focus solely on writing code without managing servers or infrastructure. Cloud Functions is well-suited for event-driven applications and microservices architectures. For containerized applications, GCP provides Cloud Run, a fully managed serverless platform that lets you run containers without the need to manage the underlying infrastructure. With Cloud Run, you can deploy containerized applications from Docker images and have them automatically scaled based on incoming requests. This makes it easy to build and deploy modern applications with the flexibility of containers and the simplicity of serverless. Data analytics is a crucial aspect of modern applications, and GCP offers a powerful PaaS solution for this purpose called BigQuery. BigQuery is a serverless, highly scalable, and fully managed data warehouse that enables super-fast SQL queries using the processing power of Google's infrastructure. It is particularly well-suited for analyzing large datasets and gaining valuable insights from your data. Machine learning is a transformative technology, and GCP's PaaS offerings include Cloud AI Platform, designed to make it easy for developers and data scientists to build, train, and deploy machine learning models at scale. Cloud AI Platform provides a range of tools and services, including Jupyter notebooks for data exploration, AutoML for model development, and custom model training and deployment using TensorFlow. It simplifies the end-to-end machine learning workflow and allows organizations to harness the power of AI in their applications. Firebase, another PaaS offering by GCP, is a comprehensive mobile and web application development platform. Firebase provides a suite of tools for building high-quality apps, including features like real-time database, authentication, cloud messaging, and hosting. It also offers analytics and performance monitoring to help developers understand user behavior and optimize their applications. Firebase is an ideal choice for mobile app development and rapid prototyping. GCP's PaaS offerings also extend to IoT (Internet of Things) with Cloud IoT Core. Cloud IoT Core is a fully managed service that enables you to securely connect, manage, and ingest data from IoT devices at scale. It simplifies the complexities of IoT device management, allowing you to focus on building IoT applications and solutions. Additionally, GCP provides a wide range of PaaS offerings for data storage and databases. Cloud Storage is a scalable object storage service that allows you to store and retrieve any amount of data from anywhere on the web. It is suitable for storing unstructured data, backups, and multimedia content. Cloud SQL, on the other hand, is a fully managed relational database service that supports popular database engines like MySQL, PostgreSQL, and SQL Server. It takes care of database management tasks such as patching, backups, and scaling, allowing developers to focus on database design and application development. For NoSQL databases, GCP offers Cloud Firestore and Cloud Bigtable. Firestore is a serverless, highly scalable NoSQL database for mobile and web applications, offering real-time synchronization and offline data access. Cloud Bigtable, on the other hand, is a fully managed, highly scalable NoSQL database designed for large-scale, analytical workloads. It is suitable for applications that require high-throughput and low-latency access to large datasets. GCP's PaaS offerings also include services for identity and access management, such as Cloud Identity Platform and Cloud IAM. These services help organizations manage user identities, permissions, and access control within their applications and systems. In summary, GCP's PaaS offerings encompass a wide range of services designed to simplify application development, deployment, and management across various use cases. From web and mobile application development with App Engine and Firebase to serverless computing with Cloud Functions and Cloud Run, GCP provides tools that empower developers to focus on coding rather than infrastructure. For data analytics and machine learning, services like BigQuery and Cloud AI Platform offer powerful capabilities. Additionally, GCP's PaaS offerings cover data storage and databases, IoT, identity management, and much more, making it a comprehensive platform for building modern, cloud-native applications. Practical applications of Google Cloud Platform (GCP) Platform as a Service (PaaS) solutions span a wide spectrum of industries and use cases, showcasing the versatility and utility of these cloud-based tools. In the world of e-commerce, for instance, GCP's PaaS offerings can be harnessed to build and maintain high-performance web applications that handle heavy traffic during peak shopping seasons. Retailers can use Google App Engine to create scalable and responsive web applications that ensure a seamless shopping experience for customers. The auto-scaling capabilities of App

Engine allow these applications to dynamically adjust to fluctuating demand, eliminating concerns about traffic spikes causing downtime. In the financial sector, GCP's PaaS solutions play a crucial role in enabling real-time data analysis and fraud detection. Banks and financial institutions can leverage the power of Google Cloud's BigQuery to process vast volumes of transaction data rapidly. By executing complex SQL queries at lightning speed, BigQuery helps identify suspicious activities and potential fraud in real-time, safeguarding the financial interests of both institutions and customers. Healthcare organizations can benefit from GCP's PaaS offerings by developing secure and compliant healthcare applications. Google Cloud's healthcare-specific solutions, such as Healthcare API and Cloud Healthcare Consent Management API, enable the secure exchange of patient data and the management of patient consent. These tools help healthcare providers and researchers streamline data sharing and compliance with healthcare regulations, ultimately improving patient care and research outcomes. In the media and entertainment industry, GCP's PaaS solutions empower companies to deliver high-quality streaming services to a global audience. Media streaming platforms can utilize Google Cloud's storage and content delivery solutions, such as Cloud Storage and Content Delivery Network (CDN), to efficiently store and deliver video content. The scalable infrastructure ensures smooth streaming experiences, even during live events with massive viewership. For manufacturers, the Internet of Things (IoT) presents an opportunity to enhance operations and gain real-time insights. GCP's PaaS offering, Cloud IoT Core, facilitates the secure and scalable connection of IoT devices to the cloud. Manufacturers can collect data from sensors and devices on the factory floor, analyze it using Cloud IoT Core, and use the insights to optimize production processes and minimize downtime. In the travel and hospitality industry, GCP's PaaS solutions enable companies to offer personalized experiences to their customers. Travel booking platforms can use Google Cloud's machine learning capabilities, such as AI Platform, to analyze customer preferences and booking history. By providing personalized recommendations and offers, these platforms can increase customer loyalty and satisfaction. For educational institutions, GCP's PaaS solutions support modern online learning experiences. With Google App Engine, universities and e-learning platforms can develop scalable and interactive educational applications. These applications can provide real-time feedback, quizzes, and collaboration features, enhancing the online learning experience for students. The gaming industry benefits from GCP's PaaS solutions to deliver multiplayer and cloud gaming experiences. Game developers can use Google Cloud's managed Kubernetes service, GKE Autopilot, to deploy and manage game servers with ease. This ensures that players can enjoy smooth and responsive gaming experiences, whether playing on their PCs, consoles, or mobile devices. Public sector organizations, including government agencies, can leverage GCP's PaaS solutions to improve citizen services and enhance efficiency. By using Google App Engine and Google Kubernetes Engine

(GKE), these organizations can build and deploy citizen-facing applications and internal systems that are secure, scalable, and cost-effective. This allows government agencies to better serve their constituents and streamline their operations. In the field of scientific research, GCP's PaaS solutions offer powerful tools for data analysis and collaboration. Research institutions can use BigQuery and Google Colab (a Jupyter notebook environment) to analyze large datasets and conduct data-driven research. These tools promote collaboration among researchers by enabling them to work on the same data and notebooks simultaneously, accelerating scientific discoveries. GCP's PaaS offerings also support the development of smart cities and IoT-based urban solutions. Cities can utilize Cloud IoT Core and other GCP services to collect and analyze data from various sensors, such as traffic cameras and environmental monitors. This data can be used to optimize traffic management, reduce energy consumption, and improve public safety. In the field of agriculture, GCP's PaaS solutions aid farmers in optimizing crop yields and reducing resource waste. Farmers can use IoT devices and Cloud IoT Core to monitor soil conditions, weather, and irrigation systems. By analyzing this data, they can make informed decisions about when and how much to irrigate, ultimately conserving water and increasing crop productivity. In the energy sector, GCP's PaaS offerings help companies manage and optimize their energy resources. Utility providers can use Google Cloud's data analytics capabilities to monitor energy consumption patterns and identify opportunities for energy *conservation. These insights can lead to more efficient energy distribution and reduced environmental impact. In summary, the practical applications of GCP's PaaS solutions are diverse and span numerous industries and use cases. From e-commerce and finance to healthcare, media, education, gaming, public sector, research, smart cities, agriculture, and energy, GCP's PaaS offerings empower organizations to innovate, streamline operations, and deliver value to their customers and constituents. By harnessing the capabilities of GCP's PaaS solutions, businesses and institutions can stay competitive, drive efficiency, and meet the evolving needs of the digital age.*

Chapter 4: Deep Dive into Microsoft Azure PaaS Offerings

Microsoft Azure's Platform as a Service (PaaS) offerings encompass a wide range of use cases and bring numerous benefits to organizations across various industries. One prominent use case for Azure PaaS is web application development and hosting. Organizations can use Azure App Service, a fully managed platform, to build, deploy, and scale web applications with ease. App Service supports multiple programming languages and frameworks, allowing developers to choose the tools they are most comfortable with. The benefit here is that developers can focus on writing code and delivering features rather than managing infrastructure. Another critical use case is data storage and analytics. Azure offers Azure SQL Database, a managed relational database service, and Azure Cosmos DB, a globally distributed, multi-model database service. These services cater to a wide range of data storage needs, from structured data in SQL databases to semi-structured and unstructured data in NoSQL databases. Additionally, Azure provides services like Azure Data Factory and Azure Databricks for data integration and analytics, enabling organizations to gain valuable insights from their data. Machine learning and artificial intelligence (AI) are rapidly becoming integral to many applications, and Azure offers Azure Machine Learning, a PaaS solution for building, training, and *deploying machine learning models. Developers and data scientists can leverage this service to create predictive and analytical models, which can be seamlessly integrated into their applications to make data-driven decisions. Azure PaaS also supports DevOps and application lifecycle management. Azure DevOps Services, a comprehensive set of development tools and services, enables teams to plan, develop, test, and deliver software efficiently. It provides features like version control, continuous integration and delivery (CI/CD), and release management. This makes it possible for organizations to adopt DevOps practices and accelerate their software development processes. For content management and collaboration, organizations can use Azure Content Delivery Network (CDN) and Azure SharePoint, respectively. Azure CDN enables the efficient delivery of web content to users around the world, improving website performance and user experience. Azure SharePoint, on the other hand, facilitates document management, team collaboration, and workflow automation. These services help organizations enhance productivity and streamline content-related tasks. Azure PaaS is also well-suited for Internet of Things (IoT) applications. Azure IoT Hub, a fully managed service, allows organizations to connect, monitor, and manage IoT devices securely. With Azure IoT Hub, organizations can collect and analyze data from IoT devices, enabling them to make informed decisions, optimize operations, and create innovative IoT solutions. Additionally, Azure Functions, a serverless compute service, can be used for event-driven IoT* scenarios, where code is executed in response to IoT device events. Serverless computing is another significant use case for Azure PaaS. Azure Functions and Azure Logic Apps enable developers to build event-driven, serverless applications. These applications automatically scale based on demand and execute code in response to events, such as HTTP requests, database changes, or IoT device messages. The pay-as-you-go model of serverless computing helps organizations save costs by eliminating the need to provision and manage servers. For mobile application development, Azure PaaS offers Azure Mobile Apps, a service that simplifies backend development for mobile applications. Developers can easily add features like authentication, offline data synchronization, and push notifications to their mobile apps, enhancing the user experience. Moreover, Azure PaaS provides solutions for container management and orchestration. Azure Kubernetes Service (AKS) allows organizations to deploy, manage, and scale containerized applications using Kubernetes, a popular container orchestration platform. AKS abstracts away the complexities of Kubernetes management, making it easier for organizations to embrace containerization and microservices architecture. One of the notable benefits of Azure PaaS is its focus on scalability and elasticity. PaaS services in Azure are designed to automatically scale resources up or down based on demand. This elasticity ensures that applications can handle varying workloads, from low traffic periods to sudden spikes in usage, without manual intervention. Cost optimization is another *significant advantage of Azure PaaS. With a pay-as-you-go pricing model, organizations only pay for the resources they consume. This eliminates the need for upfront capital investments in hardware and allows organizations to adjust their spending based on actual usage. Azure PaaS services also benefit from Azure's global presence, offering low-latency access to users worldwide. Azure's extensive network of data centers ensures that applications hosted on Azure PaaS services can deliver a responsive experience to users regardless of their location. Security and compliance are paramount in Azure PaaS. Microsoft invests heavily in security measures and compliance certifications to protect customer data. Azure PaaS services provide features like identity and access management, encryption, threat detection, and compliance reporting to help organizations meet regulatory requirements and secure their applications and data. Another notable benefit of Azure PaaS is its integration with other Azure services. Organizations can easily combine PaaS services with infrastructure as a service (IaaS), software as a service (SaaS), and Azure's extensive ecosystem of services. This integration simplifies complex workflows and enables organizations to build comprehensive solutions that leverage various Azure capabilities. Azure PaaS services are also backed by Microsoft's extensive support and a vibrant community. Organizations can rely on Microsoft's expertise and resources for technical support and guidance in using Azure PaaS effectively. In addition, the Azure community and documentation provide valuable insights, best practices, and solutions to common challenges. In summary, Microsoft Azure's Platform as a Service (PaaS) offerings offer a wide range of use cases and bring numerous benefits to organizations. From web application development and data analytics to machine learning, DevOps, content management, IoT, serverless computing, and more, Azure PaaS empowers organizations to innovate, scale, and optimize their operations. The advantages of scalability, cost optimization, global reach, security, and integration make Azure PaaS a compelling choice for organizations looking to leverage cloud-based solutions to achieve their goals and deliver value to their customers.*

Chapter 5: Navigating IBM Cloud's PaaS Ecosystem

Understanding IBM Cloud Platform as a Service (PaaS) components is essential for organizations seeking to harness the full potential of IBM Cloud for application development and deployment. IBM Cloud PaaS components encompass a diverse set of services and tools that streamline various aspects of the development and deployment lifecycle. One of the foundational components of IBM Cloud PaaS is IBM Cloud Foundry, a powerful platform for building, deploying, and managing applications. Cloud Foundry provides a cloud-native environment that supports multiple programming languages, frameworks, and services. Developers can leverage Cloud Foundry's flexibility to write code using their preferred languages and libraries, reducing development friction. Additionally, Cloud Foundry offers auto-scaling and load balancing features, ensuring that applications can handle fluctuations in traffic without manual intervention. IBM Cloud Functions is another integral component of IBM Cloud PaaS, designed for serverless computing. With Cloud Functions, developers can create single-purpose functions that are executed in response to specific events, such as HTTP requests, database changes, or IoT device triggers. This serverless approach eliminates the need to manage servers, allowing developers to focus solely on writing code. IBM Cloud Functions supports multiple programming languages, making it accessible to a broad range of developers. For organizations seeking containerization and orchestration solutions, IBM Cloud Kubernetes Service (IKS) is a key PaaS component. IKS enables the deployment and management of containerized applications using Kubernetes, an industry-standard container orchestration platform. IKS abstracts away the complexities of Kubernetes management, allowing organizations to take full advantage of containerization and microservices architecture without the operational overhead. IBM Cloud Databases, including IBM Db2 on Cloud and IBM Cloudant, are essential PaaS components for data storage and management. Db2 on Cloud is a fully managed relational database service that supports various database engines, while Cloudant is a NoSQL database service designed for scalable and highly available data storage. Organizations can choose the database service that aligns with their specific data needs, ensuring efficient and reliable data management. For organizations focused on data analytics and machine learning, IBM Cloud PaaS offers IBM Watson Studio. Watson Studio provides a collaborative environment for data scientists, analysts, and developers to build, train, and deploy machine learning models. With access to a wide range of data sources and machine learning frameworks, organizations can leverage Watson Studio to gain insights from their data and infuse AI into their applications. IBM Cloud PaaS components extend to integration and messaging with IBM Cloud Integration and IBM MQ. IBM Cloud Integration simplifies the integration of applications and services, enabling seamless communication between various components of an organization's architecture. IBM MQ, on the other hand, is a message queuing service that facilitates reliable and secure communication between applications and systems. These components play a crucial role in connecting and coordinating diverse elements within an organization's technology ecosystem. Security is a top priority in IBM Cloud PaaS, and IBM Cloud Identity and Access Management (IAM) provides robust identity and access control capabilities. IAM allows organizations to manage user identities, permissions, and access policies effectively. It offers features like single sign-on (SSO), multi-factor authentication (MFA), and role-based access control (RBAC) to enhance security. IBM Cloud PaaS also includes IBM Key Protect, a service that safeguards encryption keys used to protect sensitive data. Key Protect offers centralized key management, audit logging, and integration with other IBM Cloud services, ensuring data security and compliance. To facilitate collaboration and communication within development teams, IBM Cloud PaaS provides tools like IBM Cloud DevOps and IBM Cloud Continuous Delivery. IBM Cloud DevOps offers a comprehensive set of tools for planning, developing, testing, and delivering software efficiently. It supports version control, continuous integration and delivery (CI/CD), and automated testing, enabling organizations to embrace DevOps practices. IBM Cloud Continuous Delivery complements DevOps efforts by automating the deployment pipeline and promoting continuous integration. *Organizations can define deployment pipelines, track changes, and ensure consistent delivery of applications. Documentation and knowledge sharing are essential aspects of IBM Cloud PaaS, and IBM Cloud Docs offers a centralized repository of documentation and resources. Developers and teams can access documentation, tutorials, and best practices to accelerate their understanding and adoption of IBM Cloud services. Furthermore, IBM Cloud PaaS encourages a culture of learning and improvement through access to a thriving community and support resources. Organizations can engage with the IBM Cloud community to ask questions, share knowledge, and seek assistance. IBM Cloud PaaS components are backed by IBM's commitment to security, compliance, and reliability. IBM invests heavily in security measures, compliance certifications, and data protection to ensure the integrity and confidentiality of customer data. IBM Cloud adheres to industry standards and regulatory requirements, making it a trustworthy platform for organizations with stringent security and compliance needs. In summary, understanding IBM Cloud PaaS components is essential for organizations looking to leverage the platform's capabilities for application development and deployment. From Cloud Foundry for cloud-native development to serverless computing with Cloud Functions, containerization with IBM Cloud Kubernetes Service, and data management with IBM Cloud Databases, IBM Cloud PaaS offers a comprehensive set of tools and services. Integration, security, DevOps, documentation, and community support further enhance the value of IBM Cloud PaaS, enabling organizations to accelerate innovation, streamline operations, and deliver robust and secure applications to their users. Successful strategies for navigating IBM Cloud Platform as a Service (PaaS) involve understanding the platform's capabilities, aligning them with your organization's goals, and adopting best practices to leverage its potential effectively. Start by defining your organization's specific objectives and requirements for cloud adoption, ensuring that IBM Cloud PaaS aligns with your strategic goals. Consider factors such as application modernization, scalability, security, and cost optimization to determine how IBM Cloud PaaS can address your unique challenges. It's essential to conduct a thorough assessment of your existing applications and workloads to identify candidates for migration or modernization within the IBM Cloud environment. This evaluation will help you prioritize initiatives and allocate resources efficiently. Once you've defined your objectives and assessed your current environment, develop a clear migration and adoption plan for IBM Cloud PaaS. This plan should outline the steps, timelines, and resources required for a successful transition to the cloud platform. Ensure that the plan aligns with your organization's broader IT strategy and that all stakeholders are on board with the proposed approach. Consider conducting a pilot project or proof of concept to validate the feasibility and benefits of using IBM Cloud PaaS for specific applications or workloads. This pilot project will allow you to gain hands-on experience with the platform, identify any potential challenges, and refine your migration strategy before full-scale implementation. Collaboration and communication are key elements of successful cloud adoption. Engage with your development and IT teams to foster a culture of collaboration and knowledge sharing. Encourage cross-functional teams to work together on cloud initiatives, leveraging their collective expertise and ensuring that everyone understands the value of IBM Cloud PaaS. Training and skill development are crucial for a successful transition to IBM Cloud PaaS. Invest in training programs and resources to upskill your teams in areas such as cloud-native development, containerization, and serverless computing. This investment will empower your workforce to harness the full potential of the platform. Leverage the support and resources provided by IBM Cloud, including documentation, tutorials, and community forums, to enhance your understanding of the platform and address any challenges that may arise during implementation. Security and compliance are paramount considerations when navigating IBM Cloud PaaS. Implement robust security measures and compliance practices to protect your data and applications in the cloud environment. Leverage the security features and services provided by IBM Cloud, such as identity and access management (IAM), encryption, and threat detection, to enhance your security posture. Consider working with third-party security experts to perform regular audits and assessments of your IBM Cloud PaaS deployment. Cost management is another critical aspect of cloud adoption. Develop a comprehensive cost management strategy to monitor and optimize your cloud expenses. Leverage IBM Cloud's cost management tools and best practices to track your spending, identify cost-saving opportunities, and ensure that your cloud resources are used efficiently. Scalability and flexibility are inherent advantages of IBM Cloud PaaS. Design your applications and workloads with scalability in mind, allowing them to seamlessly grow or shrink based on demand. Leverage auto-scaling features offered by IBM Cloud PaaS services to dynamically adjust resources to match workload fluctuations. Regularly review and optimize your architecture to ensure that it aligns with your scalability requirements. DevOps practices play a crucial role in navigating IBM Cloud PaaS successfully. Adopt DevOps principles and workflows to streamline development, testing, and deployment processes. Leverage tools like IBM Cloud Continuous Delivery and integrate them into your CI/CD pipelines to automate application delivery. This will enable your organization to deploy updates and new features rapidly while maintaining consistency and reliability. Monitoring and performance optimization are ongoing efforts in the cloud environment. Implement robust monitoring and observability solutions to gain insights into the performance of your IBM Cloud PaaS applications. Leverage tools like IBM Cloud Monitoring and third-party monitoring services to track metrics, detect anomalies, and troubleshoot issues proactively. Regularly analyze performance data and fine-tune your applications and infrastructure to optimize resource utilization and cost efficiency. Disaster recovery and data backup are critical considerations for ensuring business continuity in the cloud. Implement a robust disaster recovery plan that includes regular backups of your data and applications. Leverage IBM Cloud's backup and disaster recovery services to safeguard your critical assets and minimize downtime in the event of a disaster. Compliance with regulatory requirements is essential, especially in highly regulated industries. Ensure that your IBM Cloud PaaS deployment aligns with industry-specific compliance standards and regulations. Leverage IBM Cloud's compliance certifications and controls to support your compliance efforts. Collaborate with legal and compliance teams to develop and maintain a comprehensive compliance strategy. Finally, regularly review and assess your IBM Cloud PaaS adoption strategy to ensure that it continues to align with your organization's evolving goals and challenges. Engage with stakeholders, gather feedback, and adjust your approach as needed to maximize the benefits of the platform. By following these successful strategies and best practices, organizations can effectively navigate IBM Cloud PaaS, harness its capabilities, and achieve their desired outcomes in the cloud environment.*

Chapter 6: Picking the Right PaaS Tools for Your Journey

Evaluating Platform as a Service (PaaS) tools and providers is a crucial step in the process of adopting cloud technology for your organization. PaaS solutions offer a wide range of services and capabilities, making it essential to assess which tools and providers align with your specific needs and objectives. The first consideration when evaluating PaaS tools and providers is the suitability of the platform for your organization's applications and workloads. Different PaaS offerings cater to various programming languages, frameworks, and application types. Therefore, it's crucial to ensure that the PaaS platform supports the technologies used in your applications and can accommodate your development requirements. Scalability and flexibility are key factors to examine during the evaluation process. A robust PaaS platform should provide scalability options that allow your applications to grow with your business and handle increasing workloads without disruption. Consider whether the platform offers auto-scaling capabilities, load balancing, and resource optimization to ensure smooth performance during traffic spikes. Ease of use and developer-friendly features are significant considerations when assessing PaaS tools and providers. A user-friendly platform simplifies the development, deployment, and management of applications, reducing the learning curve for your development teams. Look for features like integrated development environments (IDEs), code repositories, and deployment pipelines that streamline the development process. Furthermore, examine the level of support for containerization and serverless computing within the PaaS platform. Containerization with tools like Docker and container orchestration with Kubernetes can enhance the portability and scalability of your applications. Serverless computing, on the other hand, allows you to run code in a serverless environment without the need to manage servers. Evaluate whether the PaaS provider offers native support for these technologies or integrates with popular container and serverless platforms. Security is a paramount concern when evaluating PaaS tools and providers. Your chosen platform must have robust security measures in place to protect your applications, data, and infrastructure. Examine the platform's identity and access management (IAM) features, encryption capabilities, threat detection, and compliance certifications. Additionally, consider the platform's data residency and compliance options to ensure that it meets the regulatory requirements of your industry and region. Integration capabilities are crucial when assessing PaaS providers, as your applications often need to interact with other systems and services. Evaluate whether the platform offers APIs, connectors, and integration options that facilitate seamless communication with third-party services, databases, and applications. Scalability and performance monitoring tools should also be part of your evaluation criteria. Effective monitoring and analytics capabilities are essential for tracking the performance of your applications, identifying bottlenecks, and optimizing resource usage. Look for PaaS platforms that provide real-time monitoring, logging, and analytics features to help you maintain the health and efficiency of your applications. Pricing and cost management are significant considerations during the evaluation process. Understand the pricing model of the PaaS provider, whether it's based on usage, subscriptions, or a combination of both. Calculate the total cost of ownership (TCO) by considering not only the base pricing but also data transfer, storage, and additional services that may incur charges. Ensure that the PaaS provider offers cost management tools and transparency to help you track and control your expenses effectively. Service-level agreements (SLAs) and support options are essential aspects of evaluating PaaS providers. Review the SLA to understand the provider's commitment to uptime, availability, and performance. Consider the level of customer support, including response times and escalation procedures, to ensure that you receive adequate assistance when needed. Vendor lock-in is a concern that organizations should address during the evaluation process. Assess the portability of your applications and data within the PaaS platform and the ease of migrating to alternative providers or on-premises environments if necessary. Vendor lock-in mitigation strategies, such as containerization and adherence to open standards, can help minimize this risk. Community and ecosystem support can also influence your decision when evaluating PaaS providers. A strong community of users, developers, and contributors can provide valuable resources, knowledge, and best practices that support your adoption and success with the platform. Consider whether the PaaS provider has an active community, offers documentation, and promotes knowledge sharing. Compliance with industry standards and regulations is critical, especially in highly regulated industries such as healthcare, finance, and government. Evaluate whether the PaaS provider complies with relevant standards, certifications, and data privacy regulations to ensure that your applications and data remain in compliance with legal requirements. Lastly, assess the PaaS provider's track record and reputation in the industry. Research customer reviews, case studies, and references to gain insights into the experiences of other organizations that have adopted the platform. A provider's history of reliability, innovation, and customer satisfaction can serve as valuable indicators of its suitability for your organization. In summary, evaluating PaaS tools and providers requires a comprehensive assessment of various factors, including compatibility with your technology stack, scalability, ease of use, security, integration capabilities, monitoring tools, pricing, support, vendor lock-in, community support, compliance, and reputation. By carefully considering these factors, your organization can make an informed decision that aligns with your objectives and sets the stage for successful cloud adoption and application development.

Chapter 7: Building and Deploying PaaS Applications Like a Pro

Best practices in Platform as a Service (PaaS) application development are crucial for building scalable, secure, and efficient cloud-based applications. One of the first best practices is to choose the right PaaS provider and service that aligns with your project's requirements. This decision can significantly impact your application's development process and long-term success. Ensure that the PaaS provider offers the necessary tools, services, and support for your development stack and programming languages. Another essential best practice is to adopt a cloud-native approach to application development. Cloud-native applications are designed to run optimally in the cloud environment, taking advantage of PaaS services for scalability, reliability, and resilience. This approach includes using microservices architecture, containerization, and serverless computing to build modular and highly available applications. Developers should focus on decoupling application components and using APIs for communication, allowing for flexibility and easier maintenance. Security should be a top priority in PaaS application development. Follow security best practices such as implementing proper access controls, encryption, and secure coding practices. Leverage the security features provided by your PaaS provider to protect your application and data from potential threats. Continuous integration and continuous delivery (CI/CD) pipelines are essential for efficient PaaS application development. Implement automated testing, deployment, and monitoring processes to accelerate the development cycle and ensure the reliability of your application. CI/CD pipelines allow for rapid iteration and the quick delivery of new features to end-users. Performance optimization is another crucial best practice in PaaS application development. Monitor your application's performance using the tools and services offered by your PaaS provider. Identify and address performance bottlenecks, optimize database queries, and utilize caching mechanisms to ensure your application runs smoothly, even under heavy loads. Scalability is a fundamental advantage of PaaS, and it's essential to design your application with scalability in mind. Utilize auto-scaling features provided by your PaaS provider to automatically adjust resources based on demand. This ensures that your application can handle traffic spikes without manual intervention. Consider the use of content delivery networks (CDNs) to improve the delivery of static assets and reduce latency for users worldwide. Effective use of logging and monitoring tools is critical for gaining insights into your application's behavior and performance. Leverage the monitoring and analytics services provided by your PaaS provider to track key performance metrics and detect anomalies. Implement centralized logging to collect and analyze logs from various components of your application, making it easier to troubleshoot issues. Utilize application performance management (APM) tools to gain deep insights into the performance of your application's code and dependencies. Distributed tracing can help identify bottlenecks and latency issues within your application. Implement a comprehensive backup and disaster recovery strategy to protect your application and data. Leverage the backup and recovery services offered by your PaaS provider to ensure that you can quickly recover from data loss or outages. Regularly test your backup and recovery procedures to validate their effectiveness. Version control is a fundamental best practice in PaaS application development. Use a version control system (VCS) such as Git to track changes to your application's codebase. This allows for collaboration among team members, provides a history of code changes, and makes it easier to revert to previous versions if needed. Documentation is often overlooked but is a critical best practice. Maintain up-to-date documentation for your application, including architecture diagrams, deployment instructions, and API documentation. Clear and comprehensive documentation facilitates onboarding for new team members and helps troubleshoot issues more efficiently. Use containerization to package your application and its dependencies into a container image. Containers provide consistency in development, testing, and production environments, making it easier to manage complex applications. Container orchestration platforms like Kubernetes can help automate the deployment, scaling, and management of containerized applications. Ensure that your application is designed for high availability and fault tolerance. Distribute your *application across multiple availability zones or regions offered by your PaaS provider to minimize downtime in case of infrastructure failures. Implement failover mechanisms and redundancy for critical components of your application. To enhance security, follow the principle of least privilege. Grant only the necessary permissions and access rights to users, applications, and services. Leverage identity and access management (IAM) features provided by your PaaS provider to control and audit access to your application and data. Regularly update and patch your application and its dependencies to address security vulnerabilities. Stay informed about security advisories and vulnerabilities relevant to your technology stack and take prompt action to mitigate risks. Implement a robust authentication and authorization system to protect sensitive data and resources. Use modern authentication protocols and authorization mechanisms to ensure that only authorized users and services can access your application's features and data. Ensure that your PaaS application is compliant with industry-specific regulations and standards. Depending on your domain, you may need to adhere to regulations such as HIPAA, GDPR, PCI DSS, or others. Consult with legal and compliance experts to ensure that your application meets all necessary requirements. Consider the adoption of a serverless architecture for specific components of your application. Serverless computing allows you to run code in response to events without the need to manage servers. This can lead to cost savings and simplified development and operations. Lastly, foster a culture of continuous improvement and learning within your development team. Encourage knowledge sharing, peer code reviews, and retrospectives to identify areas for improvement. Stay updated on emerging technologies, best practices, and trends in PaaS application development to remain competitive and innovative. In summary, following these best practices in PaaS application development is essential for building secure, scalable, and efficient cloud-based applications. From choosing the right PaaS provider to implementing security measures, scalability strategies, and monitoring tools, these practices can help you navigate the complexities of PaaS development and deliver high-quality applications to your users.*

Chapter 8: Advanced PaaS Development Techniques

Advanced Platform as a Service (PaaS) development strategies go beyond the basics and delve into more sophisticated techniques for building, deploying, and managing applications in the cloud. These strategies are aimed at maximizing the benefits of PaaS while addressing complex scenarios and challenges. One advanced PaaS development strategy is to embrace microservices architecture. Microservices break down monolithic applications into smaller, independent services that can be developed, deployed, and scaled individually. This approach enhances agility, scalability, and maintainability. Each microservice can have its own technology stack, and teams can work on them concurrently. Another advanced strategy is to leverage containerization technologies like Docker to package applications and their dependencies into lightweight, portable containers. Containers provide consistency across different environments, making it easier to develop and deploy applications consistently. Container orchestration platforms such as Kubernetes enable automated management of containerized applications, including scaling, load balancing, and self-healing. Using serverless computing is another advanced approach to PaaS development. With serverless, developers can focus on writing code without worrying about server provisioning or management. Functions or microservices are executed in response to specific events, such as HTTP requests or database changes, and automatically scale to handle varying workloads.

Incorporating machine learning and artificial intelligence (AI) capabilities into your PaaS applications is an advanced strategy that can lead to more intelligent and data-driven solutions. PaaS providers often offer services and tools that facilitate machine learning model development and integration. These models can be used for tasks such as predictive analytics, natural language processing, and computer vision. Advanced PaaS development strategies include optimizing your application for performance and cost efficiency. This involves fine-tuning code, optimizing database queries, and implementing caching mechanisms. Monitoring and profiling tools can help identify performance bottlenecks and areas for improvement. Additionally, cost optimization strategies involve analyzing resource usage, leveraging auto-scaling, and managing cloud spend effectively. To ensure high availability and fault tolerance, consider implementing multi-region deployments and disaster recovery plans. Distributing your application across multiple regions helps minimize downtime in case of regional outages or disasters. Implementing redundancy and failover mechanisms can further enhance application resilience. Advanced PaaS development also includes adopting advanced DevOps practices. This involves automating the entire software delivery pipeline, from code commit to production deployment. Continuous integration, continuous delivery (CI/CD), and infrastructure as code (IaC) are key components of advanced DevOps in PaaS. Implementing CI/CD pipelines ensures that code changes are automatically built, tested, and deployed, reducing manual intervention and accelerating time to market. IaC enables the provisioning and management of infrastructure through code, promoting consistency and reproducibility. Security is paramount in advanced PaaS development. Implementing advanced security practices includes threat modeling, penetration testing, and security scanning tools. Utilize identity and access management (IAM) features to control access to your resources and services. Implement encryption at rest and in transit to protect sensitive data. Perform regular security audits and stay updated on security best practices. Another advanced strategy is to adopt a micro-frontends architecture, which extends the principles of microservices to the user interface. With micro-frontends, the front-end of your application is divided into smaller, independently deployable modules. This enables teams to work on different parts of the user interface without affecting the entire application. Advanced PaaS development involves optimizing your application for observability. Implement distributed tracing, log aggregation, and performance monitoring to gain insights into your application's behavior. Leverage application performance management (APM) tools to identify performance bottlenecks and troubleshoot issues. Incorporate chaos engineering practices to proactively test and improve application resilience. Advanced PaaS development also includes strategies for managing data effectively. Leverage database scaling techniques, such as sharding and read replicas, to handle large datasets and high traffic. Implement data caching and use NoSQL databases for specific use cases that require high throughput and low latency. Utilize data warehousing solutions for advanced analytics and reporting. Another advanced approach is to implement event-driven architecture. This allows your application to respond to events or messages asynchronously, decoupling components and improving scalability. Event-driven systems can be designed to handle real-time data processing, IoT applications, and event sourcing for audit trails. Asynchronous messaging patterns, such as publish-subscribe and message queues, play a crucial role in event-driven architecture. Advanced PaaS development involves managing complexity through modularization. Utilize domain-driven design (DDD) principles to define clear boundaries and responsibilities for different parts of your application. This helps manage complexity as your application grows and evolves. Implementing feature toggles and experimentation frameworks allows you to release and test new features with controlled rollouts and user feedback. Lastly, advanced PaaS development encompasses strategies for handling large-scale data processing and analytics. Leverage big data technologies like Apache Spark, Apache Hadoop, and data streaming platforms to process and analyze large volumes of data. Use cloud-based data lakes and data warehouses for storage and querying of structured and unstructured data. Implement batch and stream processing for real-time data insights. In summary, advanced PaaS development strategies go beyond the fundamentals and explore sophisticated techniques to build robust, scalable, and resilient cloud-native applications. These strategies include embracing microservices, containerization, serverless computing, machine learning, performance optimization, high availability, advanced DevOps, security, micro-frontends, observability, data management, event-driven architecture, modularization, feature toggles, and big data *processing. By incorporating these advanced practices, organizations can harness the full potential of PaaS and deliver innovative and reliable solutions to their users. Leveraging containers and serverless computing in Platform as a Service (PaaS) environments is a strategic approach to building and deploying modern applications. Containers, such as those managed by Docker, have gained immense popularity in recent years due to their ability to package applications and their dependencies into lightweight, consistent units. Containers provide developers with a standardized environment that can run consistently across various platforms, from development laptops to production servers. Containerization simplifies the deployment process and ensures that applications work the same way in development, testing, and production environments. Container orchestration platforms like Kubernetes have further streamlined the management of containerized applications, enabling automatic scaling, load balancing, and fault tolerance. By leveraging containers in a PaaS environment, organizations can achieve greater flexibility and scalability, making it easier to manage complex applications with multiple microservices. Serverless computing, on the other hand, takes a different approach by abstracting the underlying infrastructure entirely. In a serverless architecture, developers write code in the form of functions, and the cloud provider manages the execution environment, scaling, and resource allocation automatically. This allows developers to focus solely on writing code without having to worry about server provisioning, configuration, or maintenance. Serverless functions are triggered by specific events, such as HTTP requests, database changes, or timer-based schedules, and they execute quickly in response to these events. One of the primary advantages of serverless computing in PaaS is cost efficiency. Organizations only pay for the actual compute resources consumed during function execution, which can lead to cost savings compared to traditional server-based approaches. Serverless platforms also offer automatic scaling, ensuring that applications can handle varying workloads without manual intervention. By leveraging serverless in PaaS, organizations can achieve a high level of automation and rapid development, making it an attractive option for building applications that require agility and efficiency. Combining containers and serverless in a PaaS environment is a strategic approach that allows organizations to harness the benefits of both paradigms. This hybrid approach, often referred to as "containerless" or "serverless containers," enables developers to package their applications into containers and deploy them as serverless functions. This combination offers the flexibility of containerization and the automatic scaling and cost-efficiency of serverless computing. In a containerless architecture, developers create container images that encapsulate their applications and services, including all necessary dependencies. These container images are then deployed to a containerless platform that automatically manages the execution and scaling of containers as serverless functions. This approach offers several advantages. First, it allows organizations to reuse existing containerized applications and services in a serverless context without significant modifications. Developers can take advantage of the consistency and portability of containers while benefiting from the automatic scaling* and event-driven execution of serverless functions. Second, it simplifies the deployment and management of applications, as developers don't need to worry about the underlying infrastructure or orchestration. The containerless platform takes care of resource allocation, scaling, and load balancing, allowing developers to focus on writing code and building features. Third, it offers cost efficiency by only charging for the actual compute resources used during function execution. Organizations can optimize their cloud spending by leveraging serverless containers to ensure that resources are allocated efficiently. Additionally, the combination of containers and serverless computing in a PaaS environment facilitates event-driven architectures. Developers can design applications to respond to specific events, such as user interactions, data updates, or external triggers, by executing containerized functions as serverless events. This event-driven approach allows for real-time processing and near-instantaneous response times, making it suitable for applications with varying workloads and unpredictable traffic patterns. Furthermore, organizations can take advantage of the rich ecosystem of tools and services provided by both the container and serverless communities. For example, developers can use container registries, continuous integration/continuous deployment (CI/CD) pipelines, and container orchestration tools to manage their containerized applications. Simultaneously, they can leverage serverless frameworks, event triggers, and monitoring solutions for serverless functions. By combining these technologies in a PaaS environment, organizations can build versatile, resilient, and cost-effective applications that adapt to changing demands *and deliver a seamless user experience. However, it's essential to consider the specific use cases and requirements of your applications when deciding whether to leverage containers, serverless, or a combination of both in your PaaS environment. Certain applications may benefit more from the flexibility and control of containers, while others may thrive in a serverless architecture due to their event-driven nature and variable workloads. In some cases, a hybrid approach may provide the best of both worlds, allowing you to optimize resources, reduce operational overhead, and enhance developer productivity. Ultimately, the choice of leveraging containers, serverless, or a combination thereof in a PaaS environment should align with your application's goals, scalability needs, and development team's preferences. By carefully evaluating your options and considering the specific requirements of your projects, you can make informed decisions that lead to efficient, agile, and cost-effective application development and deployment in the cloud.*

Chapter 9: Scaling and Managing PaaS Environments Effectively

Scalability strategies are vital for Platform as a Service (PaaS) applications as they enable applications to handle growing workloads and changing demands effectively. Scalability is the ability of an application to accommodate increased traffic, data, or users without compromising performance. Organizations that fail to implement scalable solutions may encounter performance bottlenecks, slow response times, and service disruptions as their applications become overloaded. To address scalability effectively, PaaS providers offer a range of tools and strategies that empower developers and organizations to optimize their applications for growth. One fundamental scalability strategy is horizontal scaling, also known as scaling out. Horizontal scaling involves adding more instances of the application to distribute the workload evenly and handle increased traffic. This approach requires the application to be designed with statelessness in mind, allowing multiple instances to share the load seamlessly. Vertical scaling, or scaling up, is another strategy that involves increasing the resources of a single instance, such as adding more CPU or memory. While vertical scaling can be effective, it has limitations and may not provide the same level of scalability as horizontal scaling, which can scale almost infinitely by adding more instances. Auto-scaling is a critical feature provided by PaaS platforms, enabling applications to automatically adjust the number of instances based on real-time demand. With auto-scaling, organizations can set thresholds for traffic or resource utilization, and the platform will spin up or terminate instances as needed. This dynamic scaling ensures that the application always has the right amount of resources to handle traffic efficiently while optimizing costs by scaling down during periods of low demand. Load balancing is an essential component of scalability strategies, distributing incoming traffic across multiple instances to prevent overloading a single server or instance. Load balancers can distribute traffic based on various algorithms, including round-robin, least connections, or session affinity, depending on the PaaS platform's capabilities. Content delivery networks (CDNs) are valuable for offloading static assets, such as images, videos, and stylesheets, to reduce the load on the application servers. CDNs replicate and cache content in multiple data centers worldwide, ensuring fast and reliable delivery to users regardless of their location. Microservices architecture is an approach that can enhance scalability by breaking down applications into smaller, independent services that can be developed, deployed, and scaled separately. Each microservice focuses on a specific function or feature, allowing teams to work on them independently and scale them as needed. Microservices can communicate with each other via APIs, enabling a flexible and scalable architecture. Serverless computing, offered by many PaaS providers, simplifies scalability by abstracting server management entirely. With serverless functions, *developers write code that automatically scales in response to events or triggers, such as HTTP requests or database changes. This serverless approach ensures that applications can handle sudden spikes in traffic without manual intervention. Database scalability is a crucial aspect of overall application scalability. PaaS providers offer various database services, such as managed relational databases or NoSQL databases, that can be scaled horizontally or vertically. Caching mechanisms, such as in-memory data stores like Redis or Memcached, can significantly improve application performance by reducing the load on the database and serving frequently accessed data quickly. Global distribution, often referred to as geo-distribution or multi-region deployment, is a scalability strategy that involves replicating an application across multiple data centers or regions. This strategy reduces latency for users in different geographic locations and enhances the application's resilience by minimizing the impact of regional outages. Content delivery networks (CDNs) play a crucial role in global distribution by caching and serving content from edge locations close to users. Microservices and containerization technologies like Docker and Kubernetes can facilitate global distribution by allowing organizations to deploy and manage application components across multiple regions easily. Serverless computing also supports global distribution by automatically replicating functions across data centers. Caching is a strategy that involves storing frequently accessed data in memory to reduce the need for repeated retrieval from databases or external* services. Caching mechanisms, such as Redis, Memcached, or CDN caching, can significantly improve application performance by serving data quickly and reducing the load on backend systems. However, organizations must implement cache-invalidation strategies to ensure that cached data remains consistent with the underlying data source. Database sharding is a database scalability strategy that involves dividing a large database into smaller, more manageable partitions or shards. Each shard can be hosted on separate servers, allowing the database to handle more significant volumes of data and queries. Sharding is particularly useful for applications with rapidly growing datasets. Queue-based processing is a strategy used to handle asynchronous tasks and manage workloads efficiently. Applications can offload resource-intensive or time-consuming tasks to message queues, allowing them to be processed separately from the main application flow. Queue-based processing can enhance application scalability by distributing tasks across multiple workers or processes. Elastic scaling, a feature offered by many PaaS providers, allows organizations to automatically adjust resources, such as CPU, memory, or storage, in response to changing workloads. Elastic scaling ensures that applications have the necessary resources to handle increased traffic or data processing requirements. Organizations can define scaling policies and thresholds to guide the platform's automatic resource adjustments. Hybrid cloud and multi-cloud strategies can provide additional scalability options. By combining on-premises infrastructure with cloud resources from multiple providers, organizations can scale their applications across different environments as needed. This flexibility allows organizations to leverage the strengths of each cloud provider and accommodate diverse workloads. Scalability testing is a critical practice to validate that an application can handle expected workloads and traffic. Organizations should perform load testing, stress testing, and performance testing to identify bottlenecks, limitations, and areas for improvement in their application's scalability. Additionally, continuous monitoring and alerting are essential to ensure that applications remain responsive and performant as they scale. By proactively monitoring key performance metrics and setting up alerts, organizations can respond quickly to issues and optimize their application's scalability. In summary, scalability strategies are essential for ensuring that PaaS applications can grow and adapt to changing demands effectively. These strategies encompass horizontal and vertical scaling, auto-scaling, load balancing, microservices architecture, serverless computing, database scalability, caching, global distribution, database sharding, queue-based processing, elastic scaling, hybrid and multi-cloud approaches, and scalability testing. By implementing these strategies, organizations can achieve the scalability needed to deliver a seamless and responsive user experience while optimizing resource utilization and costs.

Chapter 10: Ensuring Security, Compliance, and Future-Proofing Your PaaS Mastery

Security measures and compliance are paramount considerations in Platform as a Service (PaaS) environments, where applications and data are hosted on cloud platforms. Ensuring the confidentiality, integrity, and availability of data and services is essential for protecting sensitive information and maintaining trust with users and stakeholders. PaaS providers offer a range of security features and tools, but it's crucial for organizations to understand their responsibilities and implement additional security measures to meet compliance requirements and safeguard their applications. One fundamental aspect of PaaS security is identity and access management (IAM). IAM enables organizations to control who can access their PaaS resources and services. Organizations should implement strong authentication mechanisms, such as multi-factor authentication (MFA), to ensure that only authorized users can access the PaaS environment. IAM also allows organizations to assign role-based permissions, ensuring that users have the appropriate level of access based on their responsibilities. Role-based access control (RBAC) is a common IAM feature that simplifies user and privilege management. Encryption plays a critical role in securing data in transit and at rest within a PaaS environment. Organizations should use secure communication protocols like HTTPS/TLS to encrypt data transmitted between clients and PaaS services. Additionally, encryption at rest should be applied to data *stored in databases, storage services, and backups. PaaS providers often offer encryption services and key management solutions to simplify the implementation of encryption. To further enhance security, organizations can implement data loss prevention (DLP) policies and monitor for data breaches. DLP policies help prevent the unauthorized sharing or leakage of sensitive data by identifying and restricting the flow of such data within the PaaS environment. Continuous monitoring for security incidents and breaches is crucial for identifying and responding to threats promptly. Organizations should set up intrusion detection systems (IDS), intrusion prevention systems (IPS), and security information and event management (SIEM) tools to detect and alert on suspicious activities. Security logging and auditing should also be enabled to maintain a record of all actions and events within the PaaS environment. Compliance with industry-specific regulations and standards is essential for organizations, especially those in highly regulated sectors such as healthcare, finance, and government. Common compliance standards include the Health Insurance Portability and Accountability Act (HIPAA), the Payment Card Industry Data Security Standard (PCI DSS), and the General Data Protection Regulation (GDPR). Organizations must assess their PaaS environment's compliance with these standards and implement controls to ensure data protection and privacy. PaaS providers often offer compliance certifications and reports to assist organizations in meeting regulatory requirements. Securing the underlying infrastructure of a PaaS environment is the responsibility of both the provider and the organization. PaaS providers are responsible for securing the physical data centers, networks, and host systems. Organizations, on the other hand, are responsible for securing their applications, data, and access to PaaS services. Security patch management is a critical aspect of PaaS security. Organizations should regularly apply security patches and updates to their applications and the PaaS services they use to mitigate vulnerabilities. PaaS providers typically notify customers of security updates and vulnerabilities related to their services. Vulnerability scanning and vulnerability management tools can help organizations identify and prioritize patching efforts. Secure coding practices are essential for building secure PaaS applications. Developers should follow security best practices, such as input validation, output encoding, and proper error handling, to prevent common vulnerabilities like cross-site scripting (XSS), SQL injection, and security misconfigurations. Static and dynamic code analysis tools can help identify and address security flaws during the development process. Container security is crucial if an organization uses containerization technologies like Docker in its PaaS environment. Containers should be built from secure base images, scanned for vulnerabilities, and configured with the principle of least privilege. Container orchestration platforms like Kubernetes offer security features such as network policies and role-based access control (RBAC) to further enhance container security. Serverless security requires organizations to focus on securing the code and configurations of serverless functions. Access controls and authentication mechanisms should be in place to ensure that only authorized entities can trigger and invoke functions. Organizations should also monitor and log function executions to detect and* respond to security incidents. Cloud-native security solutions, such as cloud security posture management (CSPM) and cloud workload protection platforms (CWPP), can provide comprehensive security and compliance visibility across a PaaS environment. These solutions help organizations identify misconfigurations, vulnerabilities, and compliance violations and provide recommendations for remediation. Security policies and incident response plans should be documented, tested, and regularly updated to address security threats and breaches effectively. Organizations should define roles and responsibilities for incident response, establish communication channels, and conduct incident simulations to ensure preparedness. Security awareness and training programs are essential for educating personnel about security risks and best practices. Employees should be aware of social engineering attacks, phishing attempts, and other security threats that could compromise the PaaS environment. Continuous security testing, including penetration testing and vulnerability scanning, should be integrated into the organization's security practices. Regularly testing the PaaS environment for vulnerabilities and weaknesses helps identify and remediate potential security issues before they can be exploited by attackers. Security automation and orchestration tools can streamline security operations and response by automating repetitive tasks and orchestrating incident response workflows. By leveraging automation, organizations can respond to security incidents more efficiently and reduce manual errors. Security in a PaaS environment is an ongoing effort that requires vigilance and adaptability. Threat landscapes evolve, and new *vulnerabilities emerge regularly, making it crucial for organizations to stay informed about emerging threats and security best practices. Collaboration with the PaaS provider and adherence to security recommendations and guidelines are essential for maintaining a secure PaaS environment. In summary, security measures and compliance are essential considerations in Platform as a Service (PaaS) environments. Organizations must implement robust identity and access management, encryption, data loss prevention, and monitoring practices to protect their PaaS applications and data. Compliance with industry-specific regulations and standards is vital, as is the continuous management of security patches, secure coding practices, container security, and serverless security. Security awareness, training, and incident response planning are integral to a comprehensive security strategy. Furthermore, security automation and orchestration tools can enhance security operations and response capabilities. By prioritizing security and following best practices, organizations can build and maintain secure PaaS environments that meet compliance requirements and protect their assets effectively. Future-proofing skills in the Platform as a Service (PaaS) domain is essential in the rapidly evolving landscape of technology. The IT industry undergoes continuous transformations, driven by emerging technologies, changing business requirements, and evolving customer expectations. To stay relevant and valuable in the field of PaaS, IT professionals must adopt a proactive approach to skill development and anticipate the future trends and challenges. One of the key strategies for future-proofing PaaS skills is to maintain a learning mindset. Technology is* in a perpetual state of evolution, and those who embrace lifelong learning are better equipped to adapt and thrive. Continuous learning allows IT professionals to keep pace with the latest PaaS offerings, best practices, and security measures. Online courses, certifications, webinars, and conferences provide valuable opportunities for staying updated and expanding one's knowledge base. In addition to learning from formal sources, engaging in hands-on projects and experimenting with new technologies is crucial. Hands-on experience not only solidifies theoretical knowledge but also builds problem-solving skills and fosters innovation. PaaS providers often offer free tiers or trial accounts, enabling IT professionals to explore and experiment with their services without incurring significant costs. Furthermore, contributing to open-source projects and collaborating with peers in the PaaS community can provide valuable insights and broaden one's skill set. Another aspect of future-proofing PaaS skills is staying informed about industry trends and emerging technologies. This includes keeping an eye on market developments, following industry publications, and participating in discussions on forums and social media platforms. Understanding the direction in which the technology industry is heading can help IT professionals make informed decisions about skill development. As cloud computing continues to evolve, multi-cloud and hybrid cloud environments are becoming increasingly common. Proficiency in managing and orchestrating workloads across multiple cloud providers and on-premises infrastructure is a valuable skill set for the future. Developing expertise in cloud-agnostic tools and services, as well as cloud management and orchestration platforms *like Kubernetes, can enhance one's career prospects. In addition to multi-cloud, serverless computing is gaining momentum as a cost-effective and efficient way to build and deploy applications. Skills in serverless technologies, such as AWS Lambda, Azure Functions, and Google Cloud Functions, can open up new opportunities for IT professionals. Serverless architectures require a different mindset, focusing on event-driven and stateless functions, which necessitate a shift in development and operational practices. With the rise of DevOps and the increasing importance of automation in IT operations, skills in infrastructure as code (IaC) and configuration management are becoming essential. Proficiency in tools like Terraform, Ansible, and Puppet allows IT professionals to define and manage infrastructure as software, enabling consistent and reproducible deployments across PaaS environments. Containerization and container orchestration technologies are integral to modern application development and deployment. Skills in Docker and Kubernetes are highly sought after in the IT job market. Containers provide a standardized and portable way to package applications and their dependencies, while Kubernetes simplifies the orchestration and management of containerized workloads. Understanding container security best practices and implementing them in PaaS environments is another critical skill set for the future. Security remains a top concern in the world of cloud computing, and PaaS professionals must stay up-to-date with the latest security threats and mitigation strategies. Skills in identity and access management (IAM), encryption, vulnerability management, and compliance are essential for securing PaaS applications and data.*

Moreover, as data privacy regulations like GDPR and CCPA continue to evolve, knowledge of data protection and privacy compliance becomes increasingly important. AI and machine learning are revolutionizing various industries, and PaaS platforms offer tools and services to build, train, and deploy machine learning models. Familiarity with machine learning frameworks and PaaS-based AI services can be a valuable skill set for IT professionals. Machine learning enables organizations to extract insights from data, automate processes, and enhance customer experiences. PaaS providers offer managed AI and machine learning services that simplify the development and deployment of predictive models. The Internet of Things (IoT) is another technology trend that has a significant impact on PaaS. IoT devices generate vast amounts of data, and PaaS platforms offer scalable solutions for ingesting, processing, and analyzing IoT data streams. Skills in IoT architecture, data analytics, and edge computing can be advantageous for IT professionals looking to work in IoT-related projects. Blockchain technology is gaining traction in various sectors, including finance, supply chain, and healthcare. PaaS providers are beginning to offer blockchain-as-a-service (BaaS) solutions, allowing organizations to build and deploy blockchain applications without managing the underlying infrastructure. Understanding the fundamentals of blockchain, smart contracts, and decentralized applications (DApps) can be beneficial for those interested in blockchain PaaS development. Soft skills are equally important in future-proofing PaaS skills. Effective communication, teamwork, problem-solving, and adaptability are essential qualities in IT professionals. As

PaaS environments often involve collaboration with cross-functional teams, the ability to communicate technical concepts to non-technical stakeholders is valuable. Moreover, being adaptable and able to navigate organizational changes and shifting priorities is a crucial skill in the ever-changing IT landscape. In summary, future-proofing PaaS skills requires a proactive approach to learning, staying informed about industry trends, and developing a diverse skill set. IT professionals should prioritize continuous learning, hands-on experience, and engagement with the PaaS community. Skills related to multi-cloud, serverless computing, IaC, containerization, security, AI, IoT, blockchain, and soft skills are all relevant for the evolving technology landscape. By embracing lifelong learning and adapting to emerging technologies, IT professionals can position themselves for success in the dynamic world of PaaS.

Conclusion

In this comprehensive book bundle, "PaaS Mastery: Your All-In-One Guide To Azure Pipelines, Google Cloud, Microsoft Azure, And IBM Cloud," we embarked on a journey to explore the vast and ever-evolving world of Platform as a Service (PaaS). Across the four books, we delved deep into the intricacies of PaaS offerings provided by Azure Pipelines, Google Cloud, Microsoft Azure, and IBM Cloud.

In "PaaS Mastery: Navigating Azure Pipelines and Beyond" (Book 1), we laid the foundation for understanding Azure Pipelines and how it can streamline your application deployment processes. We covered essential concepts, best practices, and hands-on guidance to help you navigate the Azure PaaS landscape.

"Cloud Powerhouse: Mastering PaaS with Google, Azure, and IBM" (Book 2) expanded our horizons by exploring PaaS offerings from Google Cloud, Microsoft Azure, and IBM Cloud. We provided insights into how these cloud giants can empower your organization to build, deploy, and scale applications efficiently.

In "Platform as a Service Unleashed: A Comprehensive Guide to Google Cloud, Microsoft Azure, and IBM Cloud" (Book 3), we went deeper into the unique features and capabilities of each cloud provider's PaaS offerings. This book served as a valuable reference guide to help you make informed decisions about which platform aligns best with your specific needs.

Finally, in "From Novice to Pro: PaaS Mastery Across Azure Pipelines, Google Cloud, Microsoft Azure, and IBM Cloud" (Book 4), we took a holistic approach to PaaS mastery. We showcased how to leverage the strengths of multiple cloud platforms, optimize your PaaS applications, and advance from a novice to a pro in the world of cloud computing.

Throughout this journey, we explored a multitude of topics, including PaaS application development, deployment strategies, containerization, microservices architecture, hybrid cloud approaches, security best practices, compliance requirements, emerging technologies, and the future of PaaS development.

As we conclude this book bundle, it is our hope that you have gained a profound understanding of PaaS and the capabilities offered by Azure Pipelines, Google Cloud, Microsoft Azure, and IBM Cloud. Whether you are a developer, an IT professional, or a decision-maker within your organization, you are now equipped with the knowledge and skills to harness the full potential of PaaS for your projects and applications.

The world of cloud computing and PaaS is ever-evolving, and staying up-to-date with the latest trends and technologies is crucial. As you continue your journey in the realm of PaaS, remember that learning is a continuous process. Keep exploring, experimenting, and adapting to the changing landscape of technology.

Thank you for embarking on this educational journey with us. We wish you great success in your endeavors with PaaS, and may your mastery of these powerful platforms lead to innovation, efficiency, and growth in your projects and organizations.

www.ingramcontent.com/pod-product-compliance
Lightning Source LLC
Chambersburg PA
CBHW071236050326
40690CB00011B/2135